1972

This book may be kept

St

WORDSWORTH'S DIRGE AND PROMISE

Yet some with apprehensive ear shall drink
A dirge devoutly breathed o'er sorrows past;
And to the attendant promise will give heed—

from a sonnet composed while Wordsworth was "engaged in writing a tract occasioned by the Convention of Cintra."

Wordsworth's Dirge and Promise

*Napoleon, Wellington, and the
Convention of Cintra*

GORDON KENT THOMAS

UNIVERSITY OF NEBRASKA PRESS · LINCOLN

Contents

Acknowledgments   vii

Introduction   3

1 The Press Reports   11

2 Reaction to the Convention of Cintra and
   Composition of the *Cintra* Tract   31

3 Wordsworth's Intent: History or Principles?   59

4 The Doctrine of National Happiness   85

5 Poet and People, Statesmen and Generals,
   and the Doctrine of Leadership   111

6 The Results of the *Cintra* Tract   135

7 The *Cintra* Tract: Apostate's Creed?   151

   Selected Bibliography   167

   Index   175

Acknowledgments

I express my gratitude to all who have in various ways helped this study along. I acknowledge especially the following: the late George Wilbur Meyer, teacher, inspiration, and friend, for the initial encouragement to undertake the project and for wonderfully helpful direction during its early stages; Andy P. Antippas, who came to my rescue and direction upon the death of Dr. Meyer in 1967, for his wise and patient guidance and for his energetic devotion to the principle of teaching as a serving profession; John D. Husband and Purvis E. Boyette, for critical readings of early versions of the manuscript; Wallace W. Douglas and Geoffrey Carnall, for their readings of portions of the study and for their helpful suggestions; the Church College of Hawaii, for a sabbatical leave in 1966 that enabled me to begin the project; Tulane University, where most of the research that produced this study was done, for financial assistance, for a dedicated library staff whose services to me in this study have extended far beyond my stay in New Orleans, and for inspiration and guidance in every professional contact I made there; my parents, Mr.

and Mrs. Edwin Thomas, for encouragement and generous financial aid when it was needed; and my wife, M. Catherine Thomas, for typing and proofreading and never-failing encouragement and patience.

G. K. T.

WORDSWORTH'S DIRGE AND PROMISE

Introduction

In 1807 the senile monarch of Spain, Charles IV, resigned to Napoleon all rights of government in his country. Obedience to the treaty of abdication was urged upon all Spaniards by the outgoing king, by the heir apparent (later Ferdinand VII), by the Madrid Junta, and by the Holy Inquisition. Despite such counsel, the people of Spain, in a genuine popular uprising "both furious and sustained," revolted against the occupying French forces and won enough local skirmishes to attract the hopeful attention of Napoleon's enemies throughout Europe. Meanwhile in Portugal the prince regent had fled to Brazil and established there a government in exile; French troops occupied Lisbon. The revolts against the invaders which had begun in Spain quickly spread into Portugal.[1]

These Iberian uprisings were seen in England as a turning point in the struggle against Napoleon: "Up to the year 1807, he had embodied the genius and strength of Revolutionary France; and her strength (at once democratic and national) far exceeded that of the torpid and artificial States around her. But now, from motives of

[1] J. Holland Rose, *Nationality in Modern History* (New York: Macmillan Co., 1916), pp. 59-62.

3

ambition, he went out of his way to interfere with a people that only asked to be left alone; and his conduct aroused in it a hatred that nothing could quench."[2] George Canning, foreign minister in England's Castlereagh government, saw the moment as one of special opportunity demanding special policy. Although England had been at war with Spain for three years, Canning proclaimed the people of Spain "instantly our essential Ally."[3] With the only official government now functioning in Spain that of Napoleon, Canning advocated replacing the traditional practice of making treaties with monarchical governments which were out of touch with their peoples by the quite revolutionary policy of placing trust in informal but binding agreements with the peoples themselves. The cabinet agreed, and the new policy was confirmed by the king's speech of July 4, 1808.[4] The initial speech before Parliament on this policy was given by Richard Brinsley Sheridan, who saw the peninsular rebellions as allowing England the greatest opportunity "since the French Revolution for the rescue of a nation's liberty." Sheridan exclaimed: "Hitherto, Bonaparte has had to contend against princes without dignity and ministers without wisdom. He has fought against countries in which the people have been indifferent as to his success. He has yet to learn what it is to fight against a country in which the people are

[2] Ibid., p. 62. The passionate hatred of the insurgents for their French invaders sometimes led them into inhumanity, as acknowledged by Spanish historians. See José María Queipo de Llano, *Historia del levantamiento, guerra y revolución de España* (Madrid: Editorial·Hernando, 1926), p. 61.

[3] Rose, *Nationality in Modern History*, p. 62.

[4] A. W. Ward and G. P. Gooch, eds., *The Cambridge History of British Foreign Policy*, 3 vols. (New York: Macmillan Co., 1922), 1:368-69.

animated with one spirit to resist him."[5]

The Anglo-Spanish alliance was formed; in August of 1808 an English expeditionary force, united with Spanish and Portuguese insurgents, invaded Portugal. The commander of these troops was Sir Arthur Wellesley, later known to history as the duke of Wellington.[6]

These events and those which immediately followed them had a profound effect on William Wordsworth. In his seventy-third year, when he dictated to Isabella Fenwick his note on the sonnet "Written in London, September, 1802," he told her, "It would not be easy to conceive with what a depth of feeling I entered into the struggle carried on by the Spaniards for their deliverance from the usurped power of the French."[7] It is likely, as Mary Moorman has suggested, that during the time of the peninsular uprisings and the English intervention, Wordsworth relived in his imagination his exciting days in revolutionary France.[8] But the poet did not trust to feeling or imagination for information on these exciting events. His eagerness, even impatience, for news about the Spanish and Portuguese and their English allies is clear in his telling Miss Fenwick, "Many times [during the Spanish revolt] have I gone from Allen Bank in Grasmere Vale, where we were then residing, to the top of the Raise-gap as it is called [a walk of nearly ten miles altogether] so late as two o'clock in the morn-

[5] Ibid., p. 368.

[6] Ibid., pp. 369-70. Wellesley became duke of Wellington in 1810.

[7] *The Poetical Works of William Wordsworth,* ed. Ernest de Selincourt and Helen Darbishire, 2d ed. rev., 5 vols. (Oxford: Oxford University Press, 1952-59), 3:455. All references to the Fenwick notes and to poems other than *The Prelude* are to this edition, hereafter cited as *Poetical Works.*

[8] Mary Moorman, *William Wordsworth, a Biography: The Later Years, 1803-1850* (Oxford: Oxford University Press, 1965), p. 149.

ing, to meet the carrier bringing the newspaper from Keswick."[9] Lacking the kind of first-hand knowledge of events on the Peninsula that had helped him years before in forming his opinions about the French Revolution, Wordsworth relied on the descriptions of those events given in the British newspapers. His reactions ought, then, to be recognized primarily as reactions to press reports rather than to actual historical events; and it is primarily to these press reports which Wordsworth read rather than to the actual events as later historians have described them that special attention will be given, in an attempt to follow the growth of the poet's mind as he "entered into the struggle" of the Peninsula.

These reactions, however, were shaped by opinions which Wordsworth already held prior to the peninsular uprisings. He had already formed an abiding dislike for Napoleon and for what Wordsworth saw as the emperor's perversion of the French Revolution—feelings shown in such poems as "Calais, August, 1802," published January 29, 1803, in the *Morning Post,* in which he had attacked the "men of prostrate mind," the "feeble Heads, to slavery prone," who crowded eagerly "to bend the knee / In France, before the new-born Majesty,"[10] or the sonnet published in 1807 entitled "Thought of a Briton on the Subjugation of Switzerland," in which Napoleon had been called "a Tyrant" to be resisted "with holy glee."[11]

Even as his dislike for Napoleon had increased, Wordsworth seems never to have dropped certain reserva-

[9] *Poetical Works,* 3:455.
[10] Ibid., p. 109.
[11] Ibid., p. 115.

tions he had about the inhabitants of the Peninsula who were to become victims and foes of the French emperor. In 1808 and 1809, in response to the cries of Spain and Portugal for English help, he wrote the tract which he entitled *Concerning the Relations of Great Britain, Spain, and Portugal to Each Other, and to the Common Enemy, at This Crisis; and Specifically as Affected by the Convention of Cintra: The Whole Brought to the Test of Those Principles, by Which Alone the Independence and Freedom of Nations Can Be Preserved or Recovered.*[12] In writing this tract, the poet said that he regarded the Iberian peoples as moved by "exalted sentiments of universal morality" in maintaining "this most sacred cause" (*Cintra,* pp. 42-43). But he apparently still had some doubts. In a letter to William Mathews, who had visited the Peninsula, written February 17, 1794, Wordsworth had asked: "What rema[rks] do you make on the Portuguese? in what state is knowledge with them? and have the principles of free government any advocate there? or is Liberty a sound, of which they have never heard? Are they so debased by superstition as we are told, or are they improving in anything? I should wish much to hear of those things, and to know what made the most impression upon you, whilst amongst them."[13] These questionings about the possible incompatibility of liberty and minds "debased by superstition" were to reappear in the fragmentary poem, never published by Wordsworth, entitled "Pelayo,"

[12] In *Wordsworth's Tract on the Convention of Cintra, with Two Letters of Wordsworth Written in the Year 1811,* ed. A. V. Dicey (London: Oxford University Press, 1915); hereafter cited as *Cintra.*

[13] *The Early Letters of William and Dorothy Wordsworth (1785-1805),* ed. Ernest de Selincourt (London: Oxford University Press, 1935), p. 110 (hereafter cited as *Early Letters*).

whose composition Ernest de Selincourt has dated at about the time of the English intervention in the Peninsula. In the lines describing Spain under Napoleon's rule, the poet wrote:

A foreign Tyrant speaks his impious will,
And Spain hath owned the monarch which he gave.
Most horrible attempt, unthought of hour
Of human shame and black indignity!
Alas! not unprovoked these Tempests lower,
Not uninvited this malignity!
Full long relinquishing a precious dower
By Gothic virtue won, secured by oath
Of king and people pledged in mutual troth,
The Spaniard hath approached on servile knee
The native Ruler all too willingly.
Full many an age in that degenerate Land
The rightful Master hath betrayed his trust;
Earthward the imperial flower was bent
  In mortal languishment.
This knew the Spoiler whose victorious hand
Hath snapp'd th' enfeebled stalk and laid its head
  in dust.[14]

In addition to his growing dislike for Napoleon and his lingering doubts about the worthiness of the Spanish and Portuguese, Wordsworth arrived at the top of the Raise-gap in search of news from the Peninsula with a third relevant opinion already formed—his opinion about England's responsibility and England's condition. England's

[14] *Poetical Works*, 3:416.

mission, according to his sonnet "When I Have Borne in Memory," published in the *Morning Post* on September 17, 1803, remained that of "a bulwark for the cause of men."[15] But England's condition was corrupt, as Wordsworth described in the sonnet "Written in London, September, 1802," published in 1807 (and connected by the poet with the uprisings in Spain in his later comment on it to Miss Fenwick):

> No grandeur now in nature or in book
> Delights us. Rapine, avarice, expense,
> This is idolatry; and these we adore:
> Plain living and high thinking are no more:
> The homely beauty of the good old cause
> Is gone; our peace, our fearful innocence,
> And pure religion breathing household laws.[16]

Wordsworth's England, thus, was entrusted with the flame of liberty but was also burdened by her own sins. It was for these reasons, the poet told his country, that

> ... the wise pray for thee, though the freight
> Of thy offenses be a heavy weight:
> Oh grief that Earth's best hopes rest all with Thee![17]

Among these preformed opinions of Wordsworth, then, were to be planted the press reports and interpretations of events in Spain and Portugal which the poet sought so eager-

---

[15] Ibid., p. 117.
[16] Ibid.
[17] Ibid., p. 119.

ly in his nocturnal walks to meet the newspaper carrier.[18]

[18] These opinions, of course, were not original with Wordsworth. Coleridge, who along with Southey and De Quincey, formed the poet's closest circle at this time, called them "sentiments & principles matured in our understanding by common energies and twelve years' intercommunion." See his letter to Thomas W. Smith of June 22, 1809, in Earl Leslie Griggs, ed., *Collected Letters of Samuel Taylor Coleridge,* 4 vols. (Oxford: Oxford University Press, 1956-59), 3:216.

1

The Press Reports

During August, 1808, and in the months that followed, Wordsworth studied with great interest but growing alarm the reports from the Peninsula which were published in the "public journals."[1] A letter, dated January 18, 1809, from Coleridge to his friend Daniel Stuart, publisher of the London *Courier,* makes it clear that the members of the poet's circle had been following the reports in several journals.[2] Stuart's *Courier* was one of these, but it was not entirely satisfactory to all of its Lake District readers: wrote Coleridge, "What I most desiderate in the Courier . . . is steadiness & consistency."[3] But Wordsworth later published part of his *Cintra* tract in the *Courier,* for it was, as he put it, "one of the most impartial and extensively circulated journals of the time" (*Cintra,* p. 3).[4] Some of the shortcomings and unsteadinesses found by Coleridge in the *Courier* may have been because of the fact that the paper was dependent on government dispatches for its news from abroad. On the

[1] See his "Advertisement" to *Cintra,* p. 3.
[2] Griggs, *Letters of Coleridge,* 3:167-68.
[3] Ibid., p. 168.
[4] The *Courier* claimed in its masthead to have the largest circulation of any known newspaper—about 6,000 per day.

other hand, the London *Times* in these months, having been denied access to such dispatches because of its strong criticism of the ministry, had inaugurated the system of special correspondents abroad. In 1808 and 1809 the *Times* correspondent in Spain and Portugal was Henry Crabb Robinson.[5] The reports of these two papers are, thus, of great use in determining what Wordsworth was thinking and learning as he began, late in 1808, to work on his tract inspired by the Convention of Cintra. In addition, it is worthwhile to compare with the *Courier* and the *Times* such other periodicals as Leigh Hunt's *Examiner,* the strongly Whig writers of the *Edinburgh Review,* and press reports from the Peninsula and from France.

On July 4, 1808, the same day on which George III spoke to confirm the adoption of the policy advocated by Canning and Sheridan, the *Times* announced the spreading of the insurrections against Napoleon into Portugal: "In Portugal ... the people have sworn hatred to the French, and are training in the use of arms. The Spanish Proclamations have been circulated throughout Portugal. Their effect cannot be doubted."[6] And July 6 found the *Times,* in response to the king's speech, "rejoicing ... in every incident ... which shews the sympathy that must necessarily exist between this country and Spain, which is now, though late, vigorously bursting the bonds cast over her" (p. 2).

English faith in the peninsular uprisings seemed well

[5] F. P. Wilson and Bonamy Dobree, eds., *The Oxford History of English Literature,* vol. 9, W. L. Renwick, *English Literature, 1789-1815* (Oxford: Oxford University Press, 1963), p. 37.

[6] *Times* (London), 4 July, 1808, p. 2. Further page references to periodicals will be included in the text throughout this chapter.

placed when news arrived of the victory, late in July, 1808, of Spanish guerilla forces over a large French army commanded by General Pierre Dupont, at Bailén; over twenty thousand of Napoleon's troops were captured, and south and central Spain were cleared of the invaders.[7] A century and a half later, Winston Churchill described the effect of this battle thus: "Napoleon felt in every nerve and fibre the tremor which ran through Europe and jarred the foundations of his Imperial throne."[8] Wordsworth, too, felt the tremor, as transmitted through the press. On August 8, 1808, the *Times* issued an extraordinary afternoon edition of one page, exulting over the victory at Bailén as follows:

We cannot restrain ourselves from communicating to the Public, with the utmost celerity, the pleasure with which we have been ourselves transported, on receiving this moment the Official Dispatches of the two Generals Castaños and Tilli, notifying to the Supreme Junta of Seville the full surrender of Dupont, and all his forces, as well those that had not been brought into action, as those who had fought and been conquered—as well those in the plain, as those who occupied the summits and passes of the mountains, together with all their baggage, arms, ammunition, and the fruits their [*sic*] rapacity—their plunder. It is not the least gratifying article of this capitulation, they are to conveyed [*sic*] back to France by sea, a performance in which we shall prob-

[7] Ward and Gooch, *British Foreign Policy,* 1:369.
[8] Winston S. Churchill, *A History of the English-Speaking Peoples: The Age of Revolution* (London: Cassell and Co., 1957), p. 258.

ably bear some part.

Besides the spirit of being transported with pleasure, which Wordsworth, as will be seen, was to find contagious, this special issue of the *Times* emphasized and made memorable two facts about the results of the victory at Bailén: the defeated French were deprived of their plunder, and the captives were to be returned to France, probably in British ships. These two features of the triumph of Spanish insurgents, unaided by English reinforcements, were to provide the newspapers, and Wordsworth, with measuring sticks by which the next settlement arrived at with the French in the Peninsula would seem disappointingly unfavorable.

The next morning the *Times* still exulted over the news from Bailén but added some new information. At almost the same moment that Dupont had surrendered to General Francisco Javier Castaños, Joseph Bonaparte, appointed by his brother to be king of Spain, had entered Madrid. Furthermore, the *Times,* lacking access to official English dispatches and so of necessity rather vague in crediting its sources, added, "Advices, we understand, reached town yesterday, that the troops under the command of Sir Arthur Wellesley had begun to disembark on a convenient part of the coast of Portugal" where they were immediately joined by Portuguese and Spanish guerrillas. [9]

Such an announcement appeared almost an after-

[9] P. 2. The effect of Spanish encouragement and English reinforcements in Lisbon was "una revolta formidavel" which forced the withdrawal of French troops from the Portuguese capital. See Manuel Pinheiro Chagas, *Historia de Portugal,* 14 vols. (Lisbon: Empreza da Historia de Portugal, 1899-1909), 7:535.

thought. Wellesley's forces arrived just at the moment when the victory at Bailén seemed to show that Napoleon's troops were no match for the aroused patriots of the Peninsula. The English and peninsular allied army, as it marched on to Lisbon against Andoche Junot's French army, seemed destined to make perhaps its greatest contribution by its shining example. On Tuesday, September 6, 1808, the *Courier* printed an extract from a letter sent on August 23 from Obidos, along the line of march. It told of French exploits in retreat which "consisted only in plundering and massacring a disarmed population"; while "Junot pays for nothing in the villages he passes through ... the Portuguese are abundantly provided with everything .... The English carry with them 500 waggons—they punctually pay for everything. What a noble contrast!" (p. 2).

On September 3, 1808, the *Times* quoted from Portuguese papers the following proclamation, dated August 4 and signed by Charles Cotton, commander of the British fleet, and Sir Arthur Wellesley:

By the Commanders-in Chief of his Britannic Majesty's forces, employed to assist the loyal inhabitants of the kingdom of Portugal:—

PEOPLE OF PORTUGAL!

The time is arrived to rescue your country, and to restore the government of your lawful Prince.

His Britannic Majesty our most gracious King and Master, has, in compliance with the wishes and ardent supplication for succour from all parts of Portugal, sent to your aid a British army directed to co-operate with his fleet already on your coast.

The English soldiers who land upon your shore do so with equal sentiments of friendship, faith, and honour.

The glorious struggle in which you are engaged is for all that is dear to man; the protection of your wives and children; the restoration of your lawful Prince; the independence, nay, the very existence of your kingdom; and the preservation of your holy religion. Objects like these can only be attained by distinguished examples of fortitude and constancy.

The noble struggle against the tyranny and usurpation of France will be jointly maintained by Portugal, Spain, and England; and in contributing to the success of a cause so just and glorious, the views of his Britannic Majesty are the same as those by which you are yourselves animated. (P. 3)

The allied army quickly liberated Lisbon; and, on August 21, with only about half of Wellesley's troops participating, according to the *Courier,* the large French army of Portugal was decisively defeated at Vimeiro.[10] The *Times,* relying on its own correspondents, had the news of victory a day before the *Courier.* Noting that there seems to have been an unusual delay in any official communication on the subject, the *Times* ran a large headline announcing "TOTAL DEFEAT OF THE FRENCH ARMY IN PORTUGAL AND ITS OFFER TO CAPITULATE." Describing with relish the humiliation of the "great and glorious" Junot,

[10] 3 September, 1808, p. 2. *Vimeiro* is also variously spelled by English newspapers (and poets) *Vemiera, Vimiera,* or *Vimiero.*

the report added the prediction that "the capitulation will of course be such as might be expected to follow so complete a victory." The terms, however, could not yet be reported because the *Times* correspondent had left Portugal for England "as soon as the enemy had indicated a disposition to surrender" (*Times,* September 2, 1808, p. 2). The *Courier* of September 3 reported the victory of Vimeiro in dispatches received from Wellesley and from his immediate superior who had just arrived in the field at the moment of victory, Sir Harry Burrard.

There followed almost two weeks of official silence in England, during which the papers and their readers could only wonder about the terms of the French surrender. Nervousness about those terms began to turn to doubts about the surrender itself. Nor was the special supplement on the official French view of events in the Peninsula issued by the *Gazette nationale et Moniteur* in Paris, on September 5, 1808, likely to be reassuring. In a review of Spain's situation and Napoleon's conduct which was precisely parallel to the view of many English Whigs, the *Gazette* claimed that a nation long kept in ignorance and poverty by a corrupt clergy and monarchy had received through Napoleon the principles of the French Revolution; but encouraged by English spies and the same old forces of reaction, the ignorant masses of the Peninsula had risen against their French benefactors. English guilt was confirmed by the intervention of English troops whose alliance with the insurrectionists was "une conduit aussi contraire a tous les principes de la guerre." As for rumors of defeats and surrenders, the *Gazette* warned, "Tout ce que les papiers anglais ont publié sur les

17

affaires d'Espagne est faux et absurde."[11] By September 13, the *Courier* had grown sufficiently nervous to warn against believing rumors at the same time that it published an elaborate rumor itself, one which, because of its distortion of the facts which the paper eventually printed, merits quoting in full:

It is somewhat extraordinary that no advices have been received from Sir Arthur Wellesley of a later date than the 24th ult., a period of nearly three weeks. In the absence of intelligence, a variety of reports prevail; none of them probably deserving credit, for we have not been able to trace any of them to a respectable source. It is rumoured, that Junot, upon his defeat by Sir Arthur Wellesley, or rather perhaps in anticipation of such an event, had entered into a convention, or concluded a capitulation with the Portuguese Government, composed of those persons to whom the Prince Regent has consigned the direction of the Government,—upon his departure for the Brazils—to the terms of which Convention our Generals have refused to accede. Among the conditions of the singular convention, with a Government which could only resume its functions with the permission of Junot, it is stated that the Russian fleet was to be placed under the protection of the Portuguese, into whose port it had originally entered as that of a friendly power.

[11] "Relation des événemens d'Espagne," p. 983. Wordsworth had at least occasional access to the *Gazette nationale,* as his letter to De Quincey of March 27, 1809, makes clear. See *The Letters of William and Dorothy Wordsworth: The Middle Years,* ed. Ernest de Selincourt, 2 vols. (Oxford: Oxford University Press, 1937), 1:269 (hereafter cited as *Letters: Middle Years).*

Wordsworth - Raleigh

Chpt. IV Nature P. 124 - 125

Chpt. III Poetic Diction

P. 90. the properties) Words.

91

92 the neutral styleses ...

94 this poetic [?] metaphor

Upon this rumour, we must remark, that the power of the persons to whom the Prince Regent had consigned the Government, had never been acknowledged by the French—that Bonaparte having declared that the family of Braganza had ceased to reign, Junot had never suffered them to enjoy or exercise any authority—they were treated as mere private individuals, with the disadvantage which did not belong to other individuals, of being objects of greater suspicion to the French, because, known to be in the confidence of, and attached to, the legitimate Government.— The report which we have just alluded to, adds, that this Convention having been signed by the Members of the Regency, had produced a pause in the operations of our Army.

Though we have been unable to trace this rumour to any authentic source, yet we must confess that it is a manoeuvre or trick perfectly in the French character—Junot might hope by such a capitulation to get off with his plunder and save the Russian squadron, and he might think that, however we might object, we could not refuse to abide by it. Nothing to be sure would be weaker in the Portuguese Regency, knowing of our approach to their assistance, than to conclude a Convention of such a nature. The very proposal to capitulate on the part of Junot would, we should think, have made them perfectly sensible that he had no hopes of making an effectual stand against the British force advancing against him. Besides, our character as allies, and allies acting with such vigour and disinterestedness, would have dictated to

19

the Regency the propriety of entering into no terms to which we should not be a party and have given our consent. Still, if the Regency had been so ill-advised as to consent to such a convention, we should be placed in a condition of considerable delicacy. Our object in assisting Portugal is to enable the Portuguese to restore the legitimate Government.—Of course after the expulsion of the French, the legitimate Government would be restored; and the Prince having delegated the Powers of Government to certain persons, those persons would immediately assume the reins of Government. If the enemy chuse to treat with them and thus to acknowledge them as the legitimate organs of Government, could we refuse to accede to any treaty or convention which they might think fit to conclude, however we might condemn and lament it? We hope, however, that before this question reaches our readers, the rumour will be contradicted by the arrival of the intelligence of Junot having capitulated to us, who have certainly the best right to his capitulation, because we have beat him.—Yet we cannot but feel considerable regret, that, immediately after the battle of the 21st, one of our wings, which had been little, if at all engaged, was not dispatched after the retreating army, whose return to Lisbon might have been cut off, and its immediate capitulation rendered inevitable. It is said that Sir A. Wellesley was strongly for this measure—why it was not adopted we are not able to explain. (P. 2)

Clearly the distrust of the Spanish and Portuguese was widespread enough among the *Courier*'s readers to allow credence to such a rumor. The betrayal by the Portuguese of their British allies which the paper suspected may well have led the *Courier* from its initial chagrin into the great indignation displayed in its pages when the facts— that the betrayal had actually been the other way around —finally became available.

Those facts, however, first appeared in the *Courier* by way of another rumor, published on September 15. Lamenting that "still we are without any decisive news from our Army in Portugal," the paper mentioned a report— which "we do not believe"—that "a capitulation has been mutually agreed to ... that Lisbon shall be a free port; that the French troops shall be permitted to return home with their arms and their *private* property (their plunder)" (p. 3). The *Courier* insisted, however, that "this statement carries its own refutation with it—No British Officer would be a party to such a capitulation" (p. 3).

Such was the information reported in the papers right up to the eve of the government's final release of the armistice terms—rumor and doubt mingled with faith in what British officers would and would not be parties to. What those officers were truly capable of doing began to appear in the *Times* and the *Courier* on the morning of September 16. The Castlereagh government, the preceding evening, released the terms of what was to become known as the Convention of Cintra (so-called because English headquarters had been established at Cintra, although the armistice was signed at Lisbon, on August 30, 1808, more than two weeks before the armistice terms were made public in England).[12] Both papers published descriptions of the convention on September 16 and commented unfavorably. The *Times* called the conditions "very far from satisfying even the most moderate and reasonable wishes of the people of England," and added, "We can hardly refrain from shedding tears" (p. 2). The *Courier,* more indignant than tearful, found the terms "grating to the English heart and ear" and explained the reasons:

The Park and Tower Guns were fired between eight and nine o'clock. —Undoubtedly it is a matter of great and deep rejoicing, that the main object of the expedition has been accomplished, and accomplished by British arms alone, the deliverance of Portugal from the yoke of France, and the depriving the enemy of another portion of his naval means. —But here joy and congratulation cease; for it must be confessed, that the terms are not such as the public had expected. They expected from the decisive victory of the 21st, gained by a British force which had afterwards been strengtened [*sic*] by 15,000 men, that Junot would have been compelled to an unconditional surrender, and that the Russian fleet would have been added to the British Navy. But here we find the French obtaining the favourable terms of being allowed to evacuate Portugal, retaining their baggage, that is, their plunder.—They are not to be submitted to the

[12] This misnaming was unknown or ignored by Lord Byron, whose Childe Harold visited the palace at Cintra in which he supposed the convention had been signed—"Behold the hall where chiefs were late convened!/ Oh! dome displeasing unto British eye!" (canto 1, stanza 24)—and who summarized his feelings thus: "And ever since that martial synod met,/ Britannia sickens, Cintra! at thy name" (canto 1, stanza 26).

usual condition of not serving again till regularly exchanged. —No—the moment they reach France they may set out upon their march to resume hostilities against this very Portugal which they have but just evacuated—This is certainly not what the public expected—it is not that brilliant result which they had expected would have crowned the glorious battle of the 21st. (P. 3)

The full terms of the convention appeared in the papers on September 17. The *Times* commented upon them, "These are indeed most mortifying occurrences to men jealous of their country's fame and glory" (p. 3).

The *Courier* anticipated later arguments that Sir Arthur Wellesley, who was replaced in the negotiations with the French by his superiors, Generals Burrard and Hew Dalrymple, was not responsible for the unfavorable terms. The paper on September 17 printed side by side Wellesley's original armistice agreement signed just after the battle and the final convention signed on August 30. Those terms of the convention upon which Wordsworth and his friends, like many other Englishmen, were to look with disfavor, were all found in Wellesley's original terms as well; that much Wordsworth could plainly see on page 2 of the *Courier* of Saturday, September 17, 1808. Among the objectionable provisions of the Convention of Cintra that were based on Wellesley's own "Articles for a Suspension of Arms in Portugal" were the following four: (1) Portugal was treated as a prize of war to be passed from the defeated French to the victorious English, with no intervention of Portuguese officers or authorities in the making of the convention. Wellesley's articles stated that the British commander would "engage to include the Portuguese armies in this Convention" and that "the British army or fleet shall be in possession of the City and Port" of Lisbon (*Courier,* September 17, 1808, p. 2). Said the *Times,* in a remark which seems to have caught Wordsworth's eye and stayed in his mind, "The British flag was elevated as if the Portuguese had not recovered their liberty, but had been consigned over to new masters" (September 26, 1808, p. 2). (2) Those who had collaborated with the French occupation, whether Portuguese citizens or not, were excused from having to answer charges of treason or any other crime. Wellesley's articles had put it this way: "No individual, whether native of Portugal, or a country in alliance with France, or of France, shall be molested for his political conduct; they shall be protected in their persons, their properties respected, and they shall be at liberty to remove from Portugal with what belongs to them within a stipulated time" (*Courier,* September 17, 1808, p. 2). (3) The defeated French were not to be considered prisoners of war; they were to be "conveyed to France"—in British ships—where they would be free to invade the Peninsula again (p. 2). (4) The French troops were to be allowed to retain all their plunder—"arms and baggage, and all their private property of every description" (p. 2).[13]

[13] The plunder was considerable. General Junot himself, besides sending to his wife a large amount of jewelry, including a necklace valued at 350,000 francs, took with him 430,000 francs in cash and many rare treasures, including the famous St. Jerome Bible, later ransomed by Louis XVIII for 80,000 francs and returned to the Portuguese government. "Quase se pode dizer que nenhum deixou de tomar para si o indevido e de se apossar do melhor que se lhe ofereceu" (*Grande enciclopédia portuguesa e brasileira* [Lisbon], s.v. "Sintra—Convencão de 1808").

24

The response which the news of the Convention of Cintra evoked from the English public and from the Wordsworth circle will be treated in the next chapter. The press of the nation had its own response, partly a reflection of the popular mood and partly a shaper of that mood. At first the mood was despairing. "Never did such a gloom pervade the capital as pervaded it during the whole of yesterday," reported the *Courier* the day after the terms of the convention became public. "It seemed as if some great calamity had befallen the country, and instead of any one's feeling exultation at the deliverance of Portugal, the first indignant question asked by every one was, Whether such terms were ever heard of?" (September 17, 1808, p. 3). The weekly London *Observer* shared in the gloom: "The illusions of victory faded before the painful knowledge, that the glory of our arms, and the expectations of the empire, had been compromised in a Convention honourable only to the enemy" (September 18, 1808, p. 2). The *Edinburgh Review* later spoke of the same gloom as "the present hopeless state of affairs" and "the total ruin of the great cause" (July, 1809, p. 469), and eventually came to view the whole British intervention in Portugal as "the most inglorious and deplorable undertaking that ever disgraced the councils of the country" (January, 1810, p. 519).

The *Times*, by September 19, 1808, showed a lessening of the gloom; the newer mood was for finding someone to blame. The *Times* held Sir Arthur Wellesley chiefly responsible, and in an open letter to him said: "Human credulity can hardly believe that any thing so monstrously injurious to your country could have entered into the heart of the basest of her sons, and still less into yours, which we believe to be proud and imperious enough" (p. 2). The attack on Wellesley was increased when Leigh Hunt, in the *Examiner* of September 25, 1808, denounced that general's participation in the Convention of Cintra under the heading "Military Delinquency." [14] To head off the charge that Wellesley's only fault lay in obeying his superior officers, whose arrival at the battlefield, it was said, was not in time to assist in the victory but allowed them "ample leisure to mar its results," [15] the *Times* declared that "all England has been deceived in its opinion of Sir Arthur Wellesley," so it is understandable that men like Burrard and Dalrymple could be tricked by him into the Convention of Cintra (September 24, 1808, p. 2). On September 26, the *Times* and the *Courier* printed details of what had only been hinted at the day before when the Sunday *Observer* had spoken of "strong remonstrance" and "so great a degree of ferment and insubordination" among the army and people of Portugal over the convention (*Observer,* September 25, 1808, p. 2). The "insubordination," as articles in the *Times* and *Courier* on Monday clarified, resulted from the official protest against the Convention of Cintra made by the Portuguese commander Bernardine Freire de Andrade, who rejected the entire treaty and specifically denounced the four provisions already objected to by the English papers, discussed above. The *Courier* was pleased at the Portuguese reaction, although such resistance made English dishonor

[14] Lawrence Huston Houtchens and Carolyn Washburn Houtchens, eds., *Leigh Hunt's Political and Occasional Essays* (New York: Columbia University Press, 1962), p. 11.

[15] W. H. Maxwell, *The Victories of Wellington and the British Armies* (London, 1891), p. 77.

seem still greater: "There is a belief that the Conventions in Portugal will not be carried into execution; but what shall wipe away the disgrace of having consented to them?" (p. 2). The fear expressed in London papers that the English dishonor would have the additional bad effect of undermining morale among the guerrilla soldiers of the Peninsula was somewhat dispelled by reports published in the Madrid *Gaceta* throughout September, 1808, reports widely circulated in England, of continuing fervor in the popular rebellion, climaxed by the special announcement of September 27 that Joseph Bonaparte had fled Madrid. Unlike Junot in Lisbon, he had not managed to carry off his plunder, for the *Gaceta* reported that all his houses and effects, as well as those of persons devoted to him, had been seized by the Madrid Junta (p. 1).

The *Times* of September 26, 1808, published a letter from Wellesley to the bishop of Oporto, a leader in the Portuguese rebellion against the French, in which the English general said of the Convention of Cintra, "This agreement contains nothing remarkable" (p. 3). Such a comment was at best unfortunate, in view of what even Wellesley's friend and lieutenant General W. F. P. Napier was later to call "the fury of the most outrageous and disgraceful public clamor that was ever excited by the falsehoods of venal political writers,"[16] in view, that is, of the excitement caused throughout England and Europe by the convention. The *Times* thereafter was not likely to miss the kind of target which Wellesley was providing. It insisted, on September 27, that the cries of outrage in

---

[16] W. F. P. Napier, *History of the War in the Peninsula and in the South of France*, 5 vols. (New York: Franklin Hudson Publishers, 1856), 1:173.

England and allied nations against the general and his superiors would not end even when "the sentence of a Court-Martial either proved their perfidy, or confirmed the more friendly, but less prevalent suspicion of their incapacity" (p. 2). For weeks, as the preparations for the actual military court of inquiry called for by the press were made and as it took place, the papers kept up their attacks on the man whom the *Times* came to prefer not to name but called "the Negociator [*sic*] of Cintra—the Convention-maker, whose sagacity saw nothing remarkable in consigning the plunder of Portugal to the rapacity of the soldier" (September 29, 1808, p. 3). That court of inquiry, held late in November, 1808, after Wordsworth was well along in the writing of his tract, produced the general results anticipated by the *Times,* which published on November 2 its suspicions of a plot to put all the blame on Burrard and Dalrymple and keep Wellesley clear (p. 2). As the member for Hampshire, Mr. P. S. Corbett, said in Parliament, Wellesley, as shown by the long delay in releasing the terms of the Convention of Cintra, was "a person whom Ministers are anxious to screen" (quoted in the *Times,* November 4, 1808, p. 3).

It is necessary to the understanding of Wordsworth's tract on the Convention of Cintra that the press reports of the events and attitudes which caused the convention and those which resulted from it have been followed in such detail. Historians such as Hazlitt and Shand, and students of Wordsworth like R. D. Havens, have found fault with the tract because its interpretation of the events in the Peninsula does not always coincide with the view held by men of different political faith or men of later historical perspective. They have claimed that the convention, seen through eyes other than Wordsworth's, "was apparently, in its larger aspects, a wise move." [17] Wordsworth, however, never claimed a historian's accuracy. He was, as the title of his tract reveals, testing the information which he had gleaned from the press reports by "those principles" which he believed essential to freedom—principles which will be considered in detail in later chapters.

[17] Raymond D. Havens, "A Project of Wordsworth's," *Review of English Studies* 5 (1929): 320; cf. William Hazlitt, *The Life of Napoleon Buonaparte*, 4 vols. (London, 1852), 3: passim; and Alexander Innes Shand, *The War in the Peninsula, 1808-1814* (New York, 1898), pp. 38-39.

2

Reaction to the Convention of Cintra and Composition of the *Cintra* Tract

The Iberian insurrections electrified England, and the decision to send British troops to the Peninsula was at first a very popular one. Sir Walter Scott wrote of the "noble candour" with which "petty and factious considerations" were "universally" laid aside when Britain learned of the opportunity to help the peoples of the Peninsula "break through the toils by which they were inclosed, and vindicate their national independence at the hazard of their lives."[1] Robert Southey said of the effect in England of the insurrections and British intervention that "the war assumed a higher and holier character, and men looked to the issue with faith as well as hope."[2] In a letter to Grosvenor Bedford, Southey expressed the feeling that "the heart of England is with those noble people. We are not only ready, willing, and able to make every effort for them, but even eager to do it."[3] Indeed, many Englishmen were stirred by events in the Peninsula to actions comparable to the support given the republic by the In-

[1] Sir Walter Scott, *The Life of Napoleon Buonaparte, Emperor of the French*, 2 vols. (Philadelphia, 1854), 2:29.
[2] Robert Southey, *History of the Peninsular War*, 2 vols. (London, n.d.), 1:346.
[3] *The Life and Correspondence of Robert Southey*, ed. Charles Cuthbert Southey, 4 vols. (London, 1850), 3:200.

ternational Brigades and other foreign volunteers during the Spanish civil war of the 1930s.[4] Walter Savage Landor announced in a letter to Southey of August 8, 1808, that he was volunteering to go to Spain. He and two Irish companions became "the first British volunteers for the Spanish national army."[5] Landor's presence in Spain could only increase the devotion to the cause felt by his friends and acquaintances in the Lake District. Wordsworth's own excitement led him, as he said, to "enter into the struggle" of the Peninsula with a depth of feeling that he later regarded as hard for others to conceive.[6] Besides his long walks in the middle of the night to intercept the newspaper carrier, and his composition of the *Cintra* tract, evidence of his involvement in that struggle appears in at least eighteen poems included among the "Poems Dedicated to National Independence and Liberty," poems with such titles as "Spanish Guerrillas" and "Indignation of a High-Minded Spaniard."[7]

For a while, then, the feelings of Wordsworth and his friends coincided with the policy of the Tory ministry and with public opinion. But "this unanimous exhilaration was upset in September by news of the Convention of Cintra."[8] The exhilaration became instead a great outcry:

The London newspapers joined in one cry of wonder

[4] Moorman, *Wordsworth: Later Years,* p. 147.

[5] C. P. Hawkes, "The Spanish Adventure of Walter Savage Landor," *Cornhill Magazine,* n.s. 74 (1933): 556. Southey himself wrote the next month, "Had I been a single man, I should long ere this have found my way into Spain" *(Life and Correspondence of Southey,* 3:167).

[6] *Poetical Works,* 3:455.

[7] See the sonnets numbered 7, 8, 13, 14, 16, 19-32, in ibid., pp. 128-40.

[8] Geoffrey Carnall, *Robert Southey and His Age: The Development of a Conservative Mind* (Oxford: Oxford University Press, 1960), p. 86.

and abhorrence. On no former occasion had they been so unanimous, and scarcely ever was their language so energetic, so manly, so worthy of the English press. The provincial papers proved that from one end of the island to the other the resentment of this grievous wrong was the same. Some refused to disgrace their pages by inserting so infamous a treaty; others surrounded it with broad black lines, putting their journal into mourning for the dismal information in contained.[9]

The effect on the public of the news of the Convention of Cintra was explosive. The reports and interpretations published in the papers are said to have roused popular indignation to a pitch of excitement unparalleled in the nineteenth century.[10] Scott described the national feeling, in his biography of Napoleon written nearly twenty years afterward, with more detachment than he himself had been able to feel at the time. Of the reaction of the English people to the convention, he wrote: "It is their nature to nurse extravagant hopes, and they are proportionally incensed when such are disappointed. The public were

---

[9] *Edinburgh Annual Register*, 1808, p. 368. William Knight mentions the same detail in describing the reaction to the convention: "The indignation in England was so great that newspapers appeared with mourning borders, and the Ministry of the day was compelled to try the generals . . . by court martial." See his *The Life of William Wordsworth*, 3 vols. (Edinburgh, 1889), 2:127. But none of the journals discussed in chapter 1, that is, those most consulted by Wordsworth, appeared with black borders. And there never was any trial by court martial, but only an "inquiry." Incidentally, the author of the anonymously published summary of Iberian affairs in the *Edinburgh Annual Register* of 1808 was apparently Robert Southey—see Kenneth Curry, ed., *New Letters of Robert Southey*, 2 vols. (New York: Columbia University Press, 1965), 1:515.

[10] Maxwell, *Victories of Wellington*, p. 79.

never more generally united in their reprobation of any measure; and although much of their resentment was founded in ignorance and prejudice, yet there were circumstances in the transaction which justified in some measure the general indignation."[11] His more immediate response at the time of the convention, however, was to partake of the "general indignation." In a letter to William Gifford, dated October 25, 1808, in the midst of the public clamor, Scott gave as a special and compelling reason for establishing what finally became the *Quarterly Review* the prospect of "an opportunity to treat of the Spanish affairs."[12] The great dissatisfaction with the convention that was expressed by government and military leaders of Portugal and by the Portuguese people in general, dissatisfaction that the English papers were quick to report, fed the fires of popular uproar in England.[13] The Spanish general Galluzo imposed a blockade on the port of Elvas, Portugal, held by the French, an action that violated the terms of the Convention of Cintra. He stated that he could not believe such an agreement to be possible. The English general Sir John Hope was sent to dislodge him; and when this story was circulated in England, Galluzo became a popular hero there as well as in the Peninsula, and Hope another villain.[14]

Although the government inquiry into the convention, which followed in November, 1808, finally exonerated the English generals from any official guilt, Burrard resigned

[11] *Life of Napoleon*, 2:34-35.
[12] John Gibson Lockhart, *Memoirs of the Life of Sir Walter Scott*, 5 vols. (Boston: Macmillan Co., 1902), 2:96.
[13] Pinheiro Chagas, *Historia de Portugal*, 7:559-60.
[14] Ibid., p. 563.

from the army, pleading ill health, and Dalrymple and Wellesley were recalled to London. The command of British forces in the Peninsula went to Sir John Moore, who had taken no part in the Convention of Cintra. But Moore was killed in battle at Coruña in January, 1809. The command then passed back to Sir Arthur Wellesley, to the dismay of many in Portugal and England.[15] The *Edinburgh Review* expressed the opinion of many Whigs and other advocates of reform that the failure of Parliament to punish the generals, and with them the ministers responsible for the failure of English policy in the Peninsula, was proof of the need for parliamentary reform.[16] There was little that could be said, in such an atmosphere, in favor of the convention, and the main defense of each of the three generals lay in attempting to shift the blame to the other two.[17]

"Never did any public event cause in my mind so much sorrow as the Convention of Cintra, both on account of the Spaniards and Portuguese, and on our own." Thus wrote Wordsworth of his own agitation upon reading what the

[15] Maxwell, *Victories of Wellington*, pp. 80-97, 117.

[16] October, 1809, p. 235.

[17] Defenders of the convention and of the generals did arise later, after the public had tired of the case. Wrote General Napier, in his *History of the War in the Peninsula*, 2:163-64: "Party writers have not been wanting . . . to exaggerate the grounds of complaint. . . . But a convention implies some weakness, and must be weighed in the scales of prudence, not in those of justice." Shand, *War in the Peninsula*, p. 38, called the government inquiry a result of the "malice of party, acting upon popular misapprehensions and irrational annoyance." William Hazlitt, a Whig for whom Napoleon personified the virtues of the French Revolution, wrote in later years of his partisan disgust at the intervention in the Peninsula of "Great Britain, that noted bully and scold, aided by that hardened prostitute, the hireling press, and that more hardened prostitute, a ministerial majority—hawking about her contraband wares and spurious bales of iniquity, scouring the seas, and infesting the land with her officious alliance and shabby diplomacy" *(Life of Buonaparte, 3:148).*

newspapers reported after the terms of the convention were made public. And he added, "Every good and intelligent man of my Friends or Acquaintances has been in his turn agitated and afflicted by it."[18] This agitation and affliction, though nationwide, reached the poet's circle with the reading of the press reports. No doubt it grew, however, through a process of exchanging and sharing. Sara Coleridge wrote of this process as it appeared to her in her girlhood during the autumn of 1808:

> It was during this stay at Allan Bank that I used to see my father and Mr. De Quincey pace up and down the room in conversation. I understood not, nor listened to a word they said, but used to note the handkerchief hanging out of the pocket behind, and long to clutch it. Mr. Wordsworth, too, must have been one of the room walkers. How gravely and earnestly used Samuel Taylor Coleridge and William Wordsworth, and my Uncle Southey also, to discuss the affairs of the nation, as if it all came home to their business and bosoms, as if it were their private concern! Men do not canvass these matters nowadays, I think, quite in the same tone.[19]

Besides talking and pacing the floor, these men wrote. In his letters of the days following news of the convention, on the most diverse subjects, Wordsworth always managed to mention his agitation. To Richard Sharpe, M.P., the poet wrote on September 17, 1808, urging parliamentary

[18] *Letters: Middle Years*, 1:257.
[19] *Memoir and Letters of Sara Coleridge,* ed. Edith Coleridge (New York, 1874), p. 45.

action on copyrights. He added as a postscript: "We are all here cut to the heart by the conduct of sir Hew [Dalrymple] and his Brother Knight in Portugal. For myself, I have not suffered so much on any public occasion these many years."[20] To Samuel Rogers, on September 29, in a letter mostly about the care of Grasmere orphans and recent poems by Crabbe, Wordsworth added, "We are all here in a rage about the Convention in Portugal; if Sir Hew were to shew his face among us, or that other doughty Knight, Sir Arthur, the very Boys would hiss them out of the Vale."[21] In sending a prospectus of Coleridge's planned weekly *The Friend* on December 3, 1808, to their mutual friend the clergyman Francis Wrangham, Wordsworth could not resist using the blank side of the sheet. He took issue with a sermon in which Wrangham had characterized the Spanish insurgents as "devoting themselves for an imprisoned Bourbon or the crumbling relics of the inquisition." Insisted Wordsworth: "This is very fair for pointing a sentence, but it is not the truth." Instead, wrote the poet, the struggle of the Peninsula was against tyranny and perfidy and inhumanity; it was a struggle which would end in making the insurgents "a *free* people" ruled by "a limited monarch." And he added, "You will permit me to make to you this representation, for its own truth's sake, and because it gives me an opportunity of letting out a secret; viz. that I myself am very deep in this subject, and about to publish upon it; first, I believe in a newspaper for the sake of immediate and wide circulation; and next, the same matter in a

[20] *Letters: Middle Years,* 1:243.
[21] Ibid., p. 245.

separate pamphlet. Under the title of *The Convention of Cintra brought to the Test of Principles; and the People of Great Britain vindicated from the Charge of having prejudged it.* You will wonder to hear me talk of principles."[22] Apparently Wordsworth's main interest was already by this time shifting from the terms of the general's agreement to the principles by which he hoped English honor and Iberian independence could be regained.

Southey too joined in the correspondence campaign. His letters are the richest source of information not only on his own thoughts but on the activities of the Wordsworth circle right after the convention was revealed. He wrote to Landor to prevent the national disgrace from discouraging the efforts of that volunteer:

> In the height of our indignation here at the infamy in Portugal, one of our first thoughts was what yours would be. We in England had the consolation to see that the country redeemed itself by the general outcry which burst out. Never was any feeling within my recollection so general; I did not meet a man who was not boiling over with shame and rage.
>
> The Spaniards *will* be victorious. I am prepared to hear of many reverses, but this has from the beginning been as much a faith as an opinion with me; and you, who know the Spaniards, will understand on what ground it has been formed.[23]

Southey wrote that "Wordsworth's objection is to the

[22] Ibid., p. 250.
[23] *Life and Correspondence of Southey,* 3:195-96.

gentlemanliness of the Convention."[24] His own objection, by contrast, he expressed in a passionate outburst: "My cry was break the terms, and deliver up the wretch who signed them to the French, with a rope round his neck. This is what Oliver Cromwell would have done. Oh Christ—this England, this noble country—that hands so mighty and a heart so sound should have a face all leprosy, and a head fit for nothing but the vermin that burrow in it!"[25] And to Scott he wrote, "What a cruel business has this convention of Cintra been. . . . My blood boils!"[26] Southey was as indigant as the *Times* and *Courier* over the plunder carried off from Portugal by the defeated French. He told Scott of a detail not reported in the papers: "In one of the Frenchmen's knapsacks, among other articles of that property which they bargained to take away with them, was a delicate female hand with rings upon the fingers."[27]

Public meetings of protest were held in early October in various places throughout the country. One of these, held in the City of London and involving important men in the nation's financial circles, must finally have seemed to pose too great a danger to the government. The ministry banned further such gatherings in London, and the king denounced the tendency to prejudge the generals' conduct before the official inquiry could begin.[28]

[24] Carnall, *Southey and His Age*, p. 88.
[25] Ibid., pp. 86-87.
[26] *Life and Correspondence of Southey*, 3:179.
[27] Ibid. He obtained this story from his brother Tom, a lieutenant on board H.M.S. *Dreadnought*, which saw action in the peninsular intervention. See *Selections from the Letters of Robert Southey*, ed. John Wood Warter, 4 vols. (London, 1856), 2:118.
[28] *Courier*, 9 October, 1808, p. 3.

The idea of such a public meeting in Westmorland or adjoining Cumberland, however, now appealed strongly to Wordsworth and his friends. Southey wrote of their plans to Humphrey Senhouse on October 15, and his letter is interesting as well for its expression of the still growing indignation of the Lake poets against the framers of the convention:

I have had a visit this morning from Wordsworth and Spedding upon the subject of this accursed convention in Portugal. They and some of their friends are very desirous of bringing before the country in some regular form, the main iniquity of the business, which has been lost sight of in all the addresses, and of rectifying public opinion by showing it in its true light. A military inquiry may or may not convict Sir Hew Dalrymple of military misconduct. This is the least part of his offence; and no legal proceedings can attach to the heinous crime he has committed, the high treason against all moral feeling, in recognising Junot by his usurped title, and in deadening that noble spirit from which and which only the redemption of Europe can possibly proceed, by presuming to grant stipulations for the Portugueze which no government ever pretended to have power to make for an independent ally, convenanting for the impunity of their traitors, and guaranteeing the safety of an army of ruffians, all of whom, without his interposition, must soon have received their righteous reward from the hands of those whom they had oppressed. He has stept in to save these wretches from the holy vengeance

40

of an injured people. He has been dealing with them as fair and honourable enemies, exchanging compliments and visits, dining with them in the Palaces from which they had driven the rightful Lord, and upon the plate which they had stolen; he therefore has abandoned our vantage ground, betrayed the cause of Spain and Portugal, and disclaimed as far as his authority extends, the feelings which the Spaniards are inculcating, and in which is their strength and their salvation by degrading into a common and petty war between soldier and soldier, that which is the struggle of a nation against a foreign usurper, a business of national life or death, a war of virtue against vice, Light against Darkness, the Good Principle against the Evil One.

It is of importance to make the country feel this, and these sentiments would appear with most effect it they were embodied in a County Address, of which the ostensible purport might be to thank his Majesty for having instituted an Inquiry and to request that he would be pleased to appoint a day of national humiliation for this grievous national disgrace. This will not be liable to the reproof with which he thought proper to receive the City Address, because it prejudges nothing—military proceedings are out of the question; what is complained of is a breach of the law of nations, and an abandonment of the moral principle, which the words of the Convention prove, and which cannot be explained away by any Inquiry whatsoever. . . .

. . . Spedding and Calvert know many persons who

will come forward at such a meeting. Coleridge or Wordsworth will be ready to speak, and will draw up resolutions to be previously approved, and brought forward by some proper person. We will prepare the way by writing in the county papers. Here ends my part of the business, and not a little surprised am I to find myself even thus much concerned in any county affairs, when the sole freehold I am ever likely to possess is a tenement six feet by three in Crosthwaite churchyard. [29]

Southey by this time was content to leave direct action to Wordsworth and have his own say later on; to Tom Southey he wrote: "It is some satisfaction to me that I shall be able to leave upon record my opinion upon this infamous Convention, in the 'History of Portugal.' " He hoped still that a voice could be raised in the Lake District to echo the sentiments of the now-muffled voice of the city: "There is a talk of an address from this country, but Lord Lonsdale will do all that he can to prevent a meeting, or oppose anything that may be done at once. He and the ministry (all ministers alike) never wish the people to come before the King with anything except professions that they are ready to kiss his Majesty's . . . [sic]. This his Majesty is not yet tired of hearing, and would go on creating knights and giving gracious replies to the end of the chapter." In Southey's view, it was up to Wordsworth

---

[29] Curry, *New Letters of Southey,* 1:483-85. An imprecise version of this same letter appears in *Life and Correspondence of Southey,* 3:175-77. Havens, "Project of Wordsworth's," p. 322, has correctly pointed out that this earlier version is cited in still more garbled form and without indication of omissions on pp. 20-21 of an otherwise useful study referred to below, John Edwin Wells, "The Story of Wordsworth's *Cintra,*" *Studies in Philology,* 18 (1921): 15-76.

to repair the national disgrace: "If anything is done in Cumberland, here it will originate with Wordsworth: he and I and Coleridge will set the business in its true light, in the country newspapers, and frame the resolutions, to be brought forward by some weighty persons; and Wordsworth will speak at the meeting, he being a freeholder. ... God help poor England! Well might W. forefeelingly call our rulers

> 'A venal band
> Who are to judge of danger which they fear,
> And honour which they do not understand.' "[30]

Whether Wordsworth was really ever "ready to speak" he was not to be given the opportunity to demonstrate. The poets were anxious to obtain the favor of Lord Lonsdale in the project of the county meeting, but he refused to approve it or even to remain neutral.[31] The plan for a protest meeting had to be abandoned, but the scheme was yet to have an enduring result. "Nothing can be done in the way of a county meeting against Lord Lonsdale," admitted Southey to his brother Tom on November 12. And he added, "Wordsworth, therefore, is now writing a pamphlet about the Convention, which doubtless will do your heart good."[32] Southey attributed to the frustrating of the project for a county meeting Wordsworth's decision to write the *Cintra* tract. In a letter to Landor, Southey wrote:

[30] Warter, *Selections from Letters of Southey*, 2:116-17. This letter too is garbled in Wells, "Story of *Cintra*," p. 21.
[31] Havens, "Project of Wordsworth's," p. 321.
[32] Warter, *Selections from Letters of Southey*, 2:108.

We used our endeavours here to obtain a county
meeting and send in a petition which should have
taken up the Convention upon its true grounds of
honour and moral feeling, keeping all pettier considerations out of sight. Wordsworth,—who left me when
we found the business hopeless,—went home to ease
his heart in a pamphlet, which I daily expect to hear
he has completed. Courts of Inquiry will do nothing,
and can do nothing. But we can yet acquit our own
souls, and labour to foster and keep alive a spirit
which is in the country, and which a cowardly race of
hungry place-hunters are endeavouring to extin-
guish. [33]

There is considerable evidence that Southey was right
about the impulse that caused Wordsworth to begin writing the *Cintra* tract. The roots of the tract, of course,
were very deep. Coleridge wrote that the work when finished contained "sentiments & principles matured in our
understanding by common energies & twelve years' intercommunion." [34] But the supression of the city meetings,
the king's remarks on prejudging, and the failure of the
project for a meeting in Westmorland seem to have had
an immediate and decisive effect on Wordsworth's plans.
His opening sentence in the advertisement which accompanies the tract made this effect plain: "The following
pages originated in the opposition which was made by his
Majesty's ministers to the expression, in public meetings
and otherwise, of the opinions and feelings of the people

[33] *Life and Correspondence of Southey*, 3:197.
[34] Griggs, *Letters of Coleridge*, 3:216.

concerning the Convention of Cintra" (*Cintra,* p. 3). The king's accusation of prejudging must have stung, for tentative titles considered for the tract indicate that Wordsworth thought of his work in the early stages of composition as a reply to the royal charge. To Wrangham he wrote on December 3, 1808, that the title of the pamphlet on which he was already at work would be "The Convention of Cintra brought to the Test of Principles; and the People of Great Britain vindicated from the Charge of having prejudged it."[35] Dorothy Wordsworth wrote to Catherine Clarkson five days later that her brother was "engaged in a work which occupies all his thoughts. It will be a pamphlet of considerable length, entitled The Convention of Cintra brought to the Test of Principles and the People of England justified from the Charge of Prejudging, or something to that effect."[36] Although Wordsworth shifted his emphasis during the composition of the tract, as the next chapters will show in detail, he still included in the finished work a brief reply to the king's speech. The chief importance, however, of that speech in the tract remains finally that of an impetus to get the poet busy writing.

The writing itself, the most significant among literary reactions to the convention, was to be a very lengthy and complicated process. Dorothy Wordsworth described her brother early in December, 1808, as "deeply engaged in writing a pamphlet upon the Convention of Cintra, an event which has interested him more than words can express. His first and his last thoughts are of Spain and

[35] *Letters: Middle Years,* 1:250.
[36] Ibid., p. 255.

Portugal."[37] Such concentration in the household at Allan Bank seems a remarkable accomplishment in its own right; it appears hardly to have been a household conducive to thoughtful writing. The members of the household included Dorothy and her brother William, and his family, and his sister-in-law, and Coleridge and his children, and De Quincey, and servants, and part of the time even Mrs. Coleridge, who was separated from her husband but sometimes stayed for as long as a week at Allan Bank. The chimneys of the house smoked intolerably. Dorothy described the hectic, cramped, and uncomfortable conditions to Catherine Clarkson in the same letter in which she said that her brother's *Cintra* tract was occupying all his thoughts:

> I will not attempt to detail the height and depth and number of our sorrows in connection with the smoky chimneys. They are in short so very bad that if they cannot be mended we must leave the house, beautiful as everything will soon be out of doors, dear as is the vale where we have so long lived. The labour of the house is literally doubled. Dishes are washed, and no sooner set into the pantry than they are covered with smoke. Chairs, carpets, the painted ledges of the rooms, all are ready for the reception of soot and smoke, requiring endless cleaning, and are never clean. This is certainly the worst part of the business, but the smarting of the eyes etc. etc. you may guess at, and I speak of these other discomforts as more immediately connected with myself. In fact we have

[37] Ibid.

46

seldom an hour's leisure (either Mary or I) till after 7 o'clock (when the children go to bed), for all the time that we have for sitting still in the course of the day we are obliged to employ in scouring (and many of the evenings also), we are regularly thirteen in family, and on Saturdays and Sundays 15 (for when Saturday morning is not very stormy Hartley and Derwent [Coleridge's sons] come.). I include the servants in the number, but as you may judge, in the most convenient house there would be work enough for two maids and a little girl. In ours there is far too much. We keep a cow—the stable is two short field length from the house, and the cook has both to fodder and clean after the cow. We have also two pigs, bake all our bread at home and though we do not *wash* all our clothes, yet we wash a part every week, and mangle or iron the whole. This is a tedious tale and I should not have troubled you with it but to let you see plainly that idleness has nothing to do with my putting off to write to you.[38]

But despite the difficulties, work on the tract proceeded, and Dorothy told of "William and Mary (alas! all involved in smoke) in William's study, where she is writing for him (he dictating)."[39]

The initial plan, as Wordsworth mentioned in his letter to Wrangham of December 3, was to publish the *Cintra* tract "first, I believe in a newspaper for the sake of immediate and wide circulation; and next, the same matter

[38] Ibid., pp. 254-55.
[39] Ibid., p. 255.

in a separate pamphlet."[40] But the methods of publication were to prove incompatible. Newspaper publication required speed of composition and newsworthiness of content. But already the Convention of Cintra was being crowded out of the public consciousness. On the other hand, Wordsworth was determined to make the "separate pamphlet" one which would endure beyond the temporary excitement. Coleridge wrote to Daniel Stuart on December 9: "Wordsworth has nearly finished a series of most masterly Essays on the affairs of Portugal & Spain—and by my advice he will first send them to you, that if they suit the Courier they may be inserted."[41] Wordsworth was, indeed, hard at work, but as John Edwin Wells says, "The statement that the 'series' of essays was 'nearly finished' appears to be one of Coleridge's characteristic identifications of design and accomplishment."[42] Enough, however, was written for the *Courier* to accept and publish a first installment on December 27, 1808, occupying nearly three columns on page 2 of that issue.[43] The second installment was slow in appearing in the *Courier.* Wordsworth later wrote in the advertisement to the tract that "an accidental loss of several sheets of the manuscript delayed the continuance of the publication" (*Cintra,* p. 3). Actually this installment was published in nearly five columns on the first and second pages of the *Courier* of January 13. The lost pages were

[40] Ibid., p. 250.
[41] Griggs, *Letters of Coleridge,* 3:134.
[42] "Story of *Cintra,*" p. 25.
[43] The text of the first installment extends to the paragraph which ends with these words: "The first pledge of amity given by them was the victory of Vimiera; the second pledge (and this was from the hand of their Generals,) was the Convention of Cintra"--p. 13 in Dicey's edition of *Cintra.*

48

apparently done over by Coleridge—he referred in a letter to Stuart to "Wordsworth's second Essay, re-written by me, and in some parts re-composed"—and the whole probably reached the *Courier* office by January 6.[44] The delay of several more days before this section appeared in the paper was probably due to the pressures common to journalism to devote space to more current matters.[45] These pressures had been anticipated by Wordsworth. In the first paragraph of this second installment, he mentions what "we have learned from public Papers," that is, from the press reports on the defeat of the French at Vimeiro and the Convention of Cintra, reports described in the preceding chapter, and adds: "These were read by the people of this Country, at the time when they were severally published, with due impression. —Pity, that those impressions could not have been as faithfully retained as they were at first received deeply!"[46] The fickleness of the newspaper-reading public, as well as delays in the transmitting of installments caused by what Coleridge described to Stuart as "the misery of our post,"[47] forced Wordsworth to

[44] Griggs, *Letters of Coleridge,* 3:164. Coleridge's claim to have "re-written" and "re-composed" the second installment, remarks Wells, is "probably to be taken rather loosely" ("Story of *Cintra,"* p. 29). Henry Nelson Coleridge wrote to Alexander Dyce on February 6, 1836, on Samuel T. Coleridge's part in *Cintra:* "They did not think of authorship *meum* and *tuum* then. Few persons are now competent to take an account of that partnership. Indeed who wants to strike any balance?" Quoted in William Knight, ed., *Prose Works of William Wordsworth,* 2 vols. (London, 1896), 1:xiii. What is interesting about this indefinite assignment of authorship is that the partnership of *Lyrical Ballads* reappeared in *Cintra.*

[45] Wells, "Story of *Cintra,"* p. 27.

[46] *Courier,* 13 January, 1809, p. 1. The second installment in the *Courier* included pp. 13-26 in Dicey's edition of *Cintra,* ending with the promise that the continuation "will speak in its true colours and life to the eye and heart of the spectator."

[47] Griggs, *Letters of Coleridge,* 3:169.

abandon publication in the *Courier*. His advertisement to the tract explained that, after the second installment in the paper, "the pressure of public business rendering it then improbable that room could be found, in the columns of the paper, regularly to insert matter extending to such a length—this plan of publication was given up" (*Cintra*, p. 3).

By February, 1809, the decision had been made to send De Quincey to London, where he would act as Wordsworth's agent in the publication of the *Cintra* tract. The young De Quincey had become the devoted assistant of the poet. That the respect and affection which he felt for the Wordsworths was returned by them, and that his departure for London was rather sudden, unforeseen the previous December, is apparent in Dorothy's letter to Catherine Clarkson of December 8:

> Mr. De Quincey, whom you would love dearly, as I am sure I do, is beside me, quietly turning over the leaves of a Greek book—and God be praised we are breathing a clear air, for the night is calm, and this room (the Dining-room) only smokes very much in a high wind. Mr. De Q. will stay with us, we hope, at least till the Spring. We feel often as if he were one of the family—he is loving, gentle, and happy—a very good scholar, and an acute logician—so much for his mind and manners. His person is *unfortunately* diminutive, but there is a sweetness in his looks, especially about the eyes, which soon overcomes the oddness of your first feeling at the sight of so very little a man.[48]

[48] *Letters: Middle Years*, 1:255-56.

De Quincey had been with Wordsworth during almost all of the composition of *Cintra*. The two of them, often joined by others of the household, had discussed thoroughly the events in the Peninsula and the principles by whose light the tract would examine those events. De Quincey now wanted to go to London anyway, and he seems to have been very willing to serve as Wordsworth's agent. In exchange, Dorothy was to manage the painting and furnishing of De Quincey's cottage in Grasmere during his absence—a task which she reported finished late the next June.[49] He accordingly left Allan Bank on February 16 or 17.[50] The arrangement seemed a logical one at the time, but inherent in it were difficulties which would delay publication of the tract until almost the middle of 1809. Wordsworth explained the arrangement with De Quincey in a letter written to Thomas Poole at the end of May, when all the preparations for the publication of *Cintra* had finally been completed:

> Mr De Quincey . . . took his departure from my house to London; and, in order to save time and expense, I begged that instead of sending the sheets down to me to be corrected, they should be transferred directly to him for that purpose; and I determined to send the remaining portions of the MSS to him as they were finished, to be by him transmitted to the Press. This was a most unfortunate resolution; for at the time as the subject of punctuation in prose was one to which I had never attended, and had of course

[49] Ibid., p. 330.
[50] Wells, "Story of *Cintra*," p. 32.

settled no scheme of it in my own mind, I deputed that office to Mr. De Quincey. *Hinc illae lacrymae!* He had been so scrupulous with the Compositor, in having his own plan rigorously followed to an iota, that the Man took the Pet, and whole weeks elapsed without the Book's advancing a step. And, as if there were some fatality attending it, now that it has been entirely printed off full ten days, I have reason to believe it is not published! And this is owing to the Printer (I conceive) having neglected to inform Mr. Stuart that the Printing was finished; Mr. Stuart having undertaken to advertize and have it published. So that the Pamphlet has been lying ten days (and ten days at this season, and after so long delay!) like a ship in a dry dock. Now is not this provoking? But I write the account to you not for sympathy, but to clear myself from any imputations of indolence and procrastination, which otherwise you would be justified in throwing upon me. My hands in fact have been completely tied. I should the less have regretted the late appearance of the work, if I had been at liberty to employ the time in adding to its value; but in fact, as I expected its appearance every day, I abandoned every thought of the kind. I must take up with the old proverb, "What cannot be cured must be endured!"—The pamphlet was sent off to me ten days ago, and the world may perhaps not see it these ten weeks![51]

The delay, at least, was not due to slowness in

[51] *Letters: Middle Years*, 1:320-21.

composition. The last part of the basic manuscript was in De Quincey's hands within two weeks of his arrival in London. Dorothy's letter to this voluntary agent, dated February 28, asks, "Do tell us how you like the conclusion? Mary and I thought the whole was written with great dignity." But if De Quincey could have foreseen the trials ahead, he might have shuddered to read her next thought: "We as well as my Brother could not help regretting that he had not more time to reconsider it. You know he never likes to trust anything away fresh from the Brain." She added that she was enclosing "an addition to one Paragraph," and she feared that if such amendments were not rushed to London "you and he will have a great deal of trouble."[52]

Trouble there was, with Wordsworth sending numerous revisions and suggestions throughout March, April, and May. Typical is his letter to De Quincey of March 26: "I do not mean to pester you with more alterations; but two suggested themselves to me this morning which must be adopted."[53] The corrections mentioned are of the minor sort which Daniel Stuart had earlier urged Wordsworth to save for a second revised edition.[54]

Some critics have been much taken with the notion that Wordsworth, completely and self-centeredly absorbed in his writing, imposed an almost impossible and thankless burden on the admiring De Quincey and, far from being grateful for the younger man's trouble, blamed him for the delays in the publication of the tract. Wells makes much of Wordsworth's grudging impatience and ingrati-

[52] Ibid., p. 260.
[53] Ibid., p. 263.
[54] See Wordsworth's acknowlegement of this suggestion, ibid., p. 258.

tude.[55] John E. Jordan writes, "Wordsworth wanted to write for posterity, but he wanted to ride the already fast-subsiding wave of popular interest in the Convention of Cintra. On the horns of his dilemma De Quincey was nearly impaled."[56] But Wordsworth's feelings toward his agent as expressed in his letters show anything but smug ingratitude. For "the trouble and I fear vexation that has accompanied this business," he told De Quincey in March, "you have both my sincere sorrow and my zealous thanks."[57] Early in May, he ended another letter to De Quincey saying: "I cannot conclude, my dear Friend, without expressing my sincere and deep regret and sorrow that you should have had so much trouble and mortification in this business. I hope, however, you will soon be at Grasmere, when you may think of it in quiet as a traveller of a disagreeable journey which he has performed and will not have to repeat."[58] In late May, with the work finally in the printer's hands, Wordsworth reiterated his gratitude: "It is now time that I should congratulate you on your escape from so irksome an employment and give you my sincere thanks for all the trouble you have undergone."[59] Again on May 26 both William and Mary Wordsworth wrote to express their thanks and approval to De Quincey. Wrote William:

> I was reading yesterday to Mrs. Wordsworth your note on Moore's Letters with great pleasure, and ex-

[55] "Story of *Cintra*," pp. 33-34, 45.

[56] John E. Jordan, *De Quincey to Wordsworth: A Biography of a Relationship* (Berkeley and Los Angeles: University of California Press, 1962), p. 63.

[57] *Letters: Middle Years*, 1:266.

[58] Ibid., pp. 310-11.

[59] Ibid., pp. 311-12.

pressing at the same time how well it was done: upon which she observed to me, "How, then, did not you use stronger language of approbation?" When you wrote to Mr. De Quincey you merely said you were "satisfied with it." I replied that this I considered as including everything; for said I, "Mr. De Quincey will do me the justice to believe that, as I knew he was completely master of the subject, my expectations would be high; and if I told him that these were answered, what need I or could I say more?"

Mary's note shows that neither she nor her husband was oblivious or unsympathetic to De Quincey's numerous troubles over the tract: "I must take the advantage of this blank paper to express to you my congratulations upon your having at last reached the end of your labours, and to repeat at the same time what William has told you, how much pleasure your part of the pamphlet has given us. I will not say one word now about the vexations we have had in connection with the trouble it has caused you. That is all over, and I hate to repeat grievances." [60] There is no indication in any of Wordsworth's letters to others during this period that he felt anything other than sympathy and gratitude toward De Quincey. He greatly regretted the delay in the publication, but his regret did not lead him to blame De Quincey as the cause. [61]

The theory that Wordsworth was annoyed at De Quincey, and especially annoyed at his system of punctuation, has no foundation in any preserved statement of the poet himself. Coleridge, however, wrote Daniel Stuart that it was his opinion

---

[60] Ibid., pp. 316-17.
[61] The point is clearly made in his letter to Stuart of May 25, ibid., p. 313.

that De Quincey was largely at fault. On May 2, 1809, he wrote: "I both respect and have an affection for Mr. De Quincey; but saw too much of his turn of mind, anxious yet dilatory, confused from over-accuracy, & at once systematic and labyrinthine, not fully to understand how great a plague he might easily be to a London Printer, his natural Tediousness made yet greater by his zeal & fear of not discharging his Trust, & superadded to Wordsworth's own Sybill's Leaves blown about by the changeful winds of an anxious Author's Second-thoughts." And Coleridge said he knew all along that De Quincey would not work out: "I can never retract my expressions of vexation & surprise that W. should have entrusted any thing to him beyond the mere correction of the Proofs."[62] On the system of punctuation used by De Quincey in the pamphlet, a system justly defended by Wells,[63] Coleridge wrote Stuart on June 13: "The periods are often alarmingly long perforce of their construction; but De Quincey's Punctuation has made several of them immeasurable, & perplexed half the rest. Never was a stranger whim than the notion that , ; : and . could be made logical symbols expressing all the diversities of logical connection."[64] These thoughts, however, are Coleridge's own; they certainly provide no evidence for the existence of what Wells calls Wordsworth's increasing "irritation with his editor," nor for De Quincey's "distur-

---

[62] Griggs, *Letters of Coleridge*, 3:205-6. In his vexation at the tardy publication of *Cintra*, Coleridge sounds as if he had forgotten his own slow speed. His eight *Letters on the Spaniards*, which he conceived as an addition to Wordsworth's tract and of which he promised to Poole in his letter of February 3, 1809, "You will soon see [them] in the Courier," actually appeared in the *Courier* the following December and January. Griggs, 3:174.

[63] "De Quincey's Punctuation of Wordsworth's *Cintra*," *Times Literary Supplement*, 3 November 1932, p. 815. Wordsworth wrote De Quincey upon seeing the finished pamphlet, "I think, indeed, your plan of punctuation admirable." *Letters: Middle Years*, 1:317.

[64] Griggs, *Letters of Coleridge*, 3:214.

bance" and "distress." [65]

There was a flurry of panic in May, but it did not further delay the appearance of *Cintra*. Wordsworth read in an old magazine of the fining and imprisonment of Benjamin Flower, who, ten years before, had been found guilty of libel for the way he had answered Bishop Watson of Llandaff's sermon published in 1793 attacking the French Revolution. No doubt remembering his own outspoken (but unpublished) response to the bishop's address, and especially conscious of, perhaps fearful at, having written in the *Cintra* tract that the British generals in Portugal "brought upon themselves the unremoveable contempt and hatred of their countrymen" (*Cintra,* p. 98), the poet appealed to Stuart and De Quincey to check the tract for anything which might be made an excuse for prosecution. In his letter to Stuart, Wordsworth wrote: "Since it has pleased his Majesty's Ministers, to their infinite disgrace, to send Wellesley back to Portugal, and since he is now at the head of a British Army, it may be said that the Truth which I have uttered in the above passage had better be suppressed or softened down. I think so myself, but submitting to your greater experience and better judgement. I have not much fear for any other passage, but should thank you to look over the sheets with this view." [66] To De Quincey he explained that he felt guiltless of any libel, "but this I should derive no benefit from, if prosecuted." [67] Others in the Wordsworth household seem not to have been so concerned. Sara Hutchinson added a note to the foregoing letter to De Quincey in which she remarked jocularly, "We Females ... have not the least fear of Newgate—if there was but a garden to walk

[65] Wells, "Story of *Cintra*," pp. 50, 51.
[66] *Letters: Middle Years,* 1:296-97.
[67] Ibid., p. 298.

in, we think we should do very nicely—and a Gaol in the country would be quite pleasant."[68] Stuart and De Quincey decided that the passage in question was not so dangerous as to require cancelling—but Wordsworth still did not regain his calm.[69]

On May 23, 1809, the author finally saw the first copies of his tract, finally entitled *Concerning the Relations of Great Britain, Spain, and Portugal to Each Other, and to the Common Enemy, at This Crisis; and Specifically as Affected by the Convention of Cintra: The Whole Brought to the Test of Those Principles, by Which Alone the Independence and Freedom of Nations Can Be Preserved or Recovered.*[70] It was the longest single work of his life. Almost exactly six months had passed since Southey had said that Wordsworth "went home to ease his heart in a pamphlet, which I daily expect to hear he has completed."[71] The process of composing and publishing the work had proved to be far more burdensome than heart-easing. When the project was all over, Wordsworth summarized his feelings on the experience to Stuart in these weary words: "Nothing but vexation seems to attend me in this affair of the Pamphlet. . . . In fact nothing can be more unfortunate for a work of this kind than a residence so far from London, and so unfavorable to communication with the post."[72]

[68] Ibid., p. 299.
[69] See his letters to Stuart of May 25 and May 31, ibid., pp. 314, 319-20.
[70] He acknowledged receipt of these first copies in his letter to Stuart of May 25, ibid., p. 313.
[71] *Life and Correspondence of Southey*, 3:197.
[72] *Letters: Middle Years*, 1:322-23.

3

Wordsworth's Intent:
History or Principles?

In his treatment of historical events in the *Cintra* tract,
Wordsworth has been accused of being inept, inattentive,
and unfair. Geoffrey Carnall, for example, claims that
Wordsworth could have believed in the nobility of the cause
of Iberian insurrectionists and their English allies "only
by keeping aloof from the more sordid and commonplace
particulars of the insurrection."[1] General Napier implies that the opinions of those who felt like Wordsworth
could only come through blind reliance on untrustworthy
sources of information: "The national character of the
Portuguese was not then understood, nor the extent to
which they supplied the place of true reports by the fabri-
cation of false ones, generally known."[2] Dicey, who defends Wordsworth against almost everyone else, defends
the military wisdom of the English generals, particularly
Wellesley, against the poet:

> Wordsworth immensely underrated the incalculable
> advantage gained by compelling, on almost any terms,

[1] Carnall, *Southey and His Age*, p. 88.
[2] *History of the War in the Peninsula*, 1:163.

the evacuation of Portugal by the armies under the command of Junot. He also clearly did not fully realize the real and immense error of the Government in making arrangements under which Sir Arthur Wellesley should be superseded, both by Sir Harry Burrard and also by Sir Hew Dalrymple. Wordsworth possibly paid the less attention to this gigantic blunder because he seems to have imagined that all the three generals were equally responsible for the characteristics of the Convention which excited his moral indignation.[3]

Wordsworth's deficiencies as a narrator of historical facts are at times clearly evident in the tract itself, as when, for example, he admits to the easy but inaccurate lumping of the rather different situations and problems of Spain and Portugal together without distinction: "I have indeed spoken rather of the Spaniards than of the Portuguese; but what has been said, will be understood as applying in the main to the whole Peninsula. The wrongs of the two nations have been equal, and their cause is the same: they must stand or fall together" (*Cintra,* p. 13).

Whatever may be said of the defects of the tract as a reliable record of the historical events surrounding the Convention of Cintra, it is essential to understand that Wordsworth never intended it to be such a record. The convention was not Wordsworth's theme; it was his incentive. He intended his tract to "move and teach, and be consolatory to him who looks upon it. I say consolatory: and let not the Reader shrink from the word" (*Cintra,*

[3] A.V. Dicey, Introduction, *Cintra,* pp. xix-xx.

p. 15). He had little to say on the actual events which inspired the tract. His concern was with recalling his nation to observance of principles which had lately been violated by men in high places. In announcing his completion of the pamphlet, Wordsworth wrote Daniel Stuart on March 26, 1809, explaining that he had dealt at length not with events but with hopes and principles—"so that, from the proportion of space which it occupied in the work, the Convention of Cintra might fairly appear, what in truth it is in my mind, an action dwelt upon only for the sake of illustrating principles, with a view to promote liberty and good policy; in the manner in which an anatomist illustrates the laws of organic life from a human subject placed before him and his audience." The objective, he continued, was not to repeat once more the sad but well-known story of the British debacle in Portugal but to fill an alarming void: "This Country is in fact fallen as low in point of moral philosophy (and of course political) as it is possible for any country to fall."[4] Thus, the events surrounding the Convention of Cintra are chiefly important in the tract for the fact that they provided Wordsworth with a choice opportunity for a discourse on moral and political philosophy.

The author of the tract, however, naturally based his hopes for a satisfactory response to such a discourse on the popular excitement over the convention. And while the work of composition and publication of the tract dragged on, that excitement faded. So Wordsworth felt required to recount some of the events that had caused the public excitement—recount them not as an historian might but as

[4] *Letters: Middle Years,* 1:264.

they had originally reached the public, with some of the immediacy and even some of the tendency to distortion of the press reports. Wordsworth stated his intention plainly:

> Doubtless, there is not a man in these islands, who is not convinced that the cause of Spain is the most righteous cause in which, since the opposition of the Greek Republics to the Persian Invader at Thermopylae and Marathon, sword ever was drawn! But this is not enough. We are actors in the struggle; and, in order that we may have steady PRINCIPLES to controul and direct us, (without which we may do much harm, and can do no good,) we ought to make it a duty to revive in the memory those words and facts, which first carried the conviction to our hearts: that, as far as it is possible, we may see as we then saw, and feel as we then felt.[5] (*Cintra,* pp. 13-14).

Wordsworth was hampered in this attempt to re-excite

[5] Although the press reports seem clearly to have been Wordsworth's source of information for the tract, his sources of the principles it contained are not so certain. A. V. Dicey stressed the kinship of those principles to Edmund Burke—*The Statesmanship of Wordsworth* (Oxford: Oxford University Press, 1917), pp. 53-54. The influence of such French writers as Rousseau and Michel Beaupuy is claimed by Crane Brinton, *Political Ideas of the English Romanticists* (London: Oxford University Press, 1926), p. 52, and by Emile Legouis, *The Early Life of William Wordsworth,* trans. J. W. Matthews (New York: E. P. Dutton & Co., 1918), p. 227. That the principles were derived from Wordsworth's reading of Livy, Plutarch, and Cicero is argued by Jane Worthington, *Wordsworth's Reading of Roman Prose* (New Haven: Yale University Press, 1946), pp. 21-24. The debt to such English republicans as Milton, James Harrington, and Algernon Sydney is shown by Z. S. Fink, "Wordsworth and the English Republican Tradition," *Journal of English and Germanic Philology* 47 (1948): 126. And Coleridge attributed Wordsworth's principles in the tract to their "twelve years' intercommunion" (Griggs, *Letters of Coleridge,* 3:216).

the public by his limited sources of information.[6] Although there were official reports published on the debates in Parliament and the court of inquiry, as well as reports of investigations into the extent of the French plunder, Wordsworth could not get them to Grasmere in time to help him with the composition of the *Cintra* tract.[7] Several times in the tract he admitted that he relied instead on the newspapers for his information on all such matters (*Cintra,* pp. 3, 50, 152). Although he seems to have been not altogether comfortable about this heavy reliance on the press reports, the pressure of time, finally, did not allow further delay in the publication of *Cintra.* In the advertisement with which he prefaced the published tract in May, 1809, Wordsworth wrote: "I must entreat the reader to bear in mind that I began to write upon this subject in November last; and have continued without bringing my work earlier to a conclusion, partly from accident, and partly from a wish to possess additional documents and facts" (*Cintra,* p. 4). To De Quincey in London he expressed in March the same wish, destined to be frustrated until too late to help with the composition, the "wish to wait for further evidence of facts."[8] Perhaps, then, it was a mixture of intent and necessity which made the *Cintra* tract not a historical narration but a defense of principles.

Chapters 4 and 5 will examine Wordsworth's detailed

---

[6] At the same time, Wordsworth was unwilling to include in the tract sensational rumors of a type not published in the English newspapers, no matter how helpfully inflammatory, e.g., Southey's brother's tale of a lady's hand amputated for the jewelry on it (see p. 39).

[7] He wrote Stuart asking for them on February 9, 1809, but he did not acknowledge receipt of them until April 26. See *Letters: Middle Years,* 1:258, 289.

[8] Ibid., p. 267.

treatment of the two important principles of nationalism and leadership. It will be a helpful preliminary to that examination, however, to note here the poet's method of distilling enduring principles out of specific events.

One such event was the firing of the cannons in London in an attempt to inspire a public celebration on the evening of September 15—just before the terms of the Convention of Cintra were made public. (Wordsworth read of this spurious celebration in the *Courier* of the next day [see pages 22 and 23 above].) The poet saw this act not merely as an attempt to deceive the public but as a symbol of the underhand scheming and corruption of rulers to be contrasted with the spontaneous and genuine spirit of "the power of popular resistance rising out of universal reason, and from the heart of human nature" (*Cintra,* p. 51). He described the event in indignant terms: "By order of ministers, an attempt had been made at rejoicing, and the Park and Tower guns had been fired in sign of good news. —Heaven grant that the ears of that great city may be preserved from such another outrage!" (*Cintra,* p. 50). Then he described his own feelings as he studied the terms of the Convention of Cintra, with the recognition that such an agreement was void by its very nature: "One man cannot sign away the faculty of reason in another; much less can one or two individuals do this for a whole people. Therefore the contract was void, both from its injustice and its absurdity; and the party, with whom it was made, must have known it to be so" (*Cintra,* p. 97). Thus, many of Wordsworth's countrymen expected their government to repudiate the generals' agreement as an isolated error. But the poet "recollected that the persons at the

64

head of government had ordered that the event should be communicated to the inhabitants of the metropolis with signs of national rejoicing," and he realized that the same spirit which animated the authors of the Convention was "found in the very council-seat" (*Cintra,* p. 99). Wordsworth then explored the workings of the minds of "men who abandon the direct road which leads to the welfare of their country" to understand what was behind the order of public rejoicing. These men, perhaps more corrupt than conspiratorial, reasoned to themselves:

> If the act be indeed so criminal as there is cause to believe that the public will pronounce it to be; and if it shall continue to be regarded as such; great odium must sooner or later fall upon those who have appointed the agents: And this odium, which will be from the first considerable, in spite of the astonishment and indignation of which the framers of the Convention may be the immediate object, will, when the astonishment has relaxed, and the angry passions have died away, settle (for many causes) more heavily upon those who, by placing such men in the command, are the original source of the guilt and the dishonour. How then is this most effectually to be prevented? By endeavouring to prevent or to destroy as far as may be, the odium attached to the act itself. (*Cintra,* p. 100).

For Wordsworth what seemed to many only a misplaced attempt at public celebration served as a key to the corruption in England's high places.

A similar key was provided Wordsworth by the ironic

contrast between the high-sounding proclamation made by Wellesley and Cotton to the people of Portugal and their own behavior. The proclamation, which had appeared in the *Times* of September 3, 1808 (see pages 15 and 16 above), spoke of the "friendship, faith, and honour" of the English forces in Portugal and urged the insurgents to "distinguished examples of fortitude and constancy." The poet asked, "Where were the fortitude and constancy of the teachers?" (*Cintra,* p. 54). He recounted the various fears later offered as excuses for the English commanders: "fear of an open beach and of equinoctial gales for the shipping; fear that reinforcements could not be landed; fear of famine;—fear of every thing but dishonour!" (*Cintra,* p. 53). He compared the known weaknesses of the French and the allied forces. And he concluded that the English leaders lacked not military courage but something far more essential. These were not "bold, bad men," but flimsy, mediocre men whose abilities and strength of character fell immensely short of their opportunities and duties:

> Let me not be misunderstood. While I am thus forced to repeat things, which were uttered or thought of these men in reference to their military conduct, as heads of that army, it is needless to add, that their personal courage is in no wise implicated in the charge brought against them. But, in the name of my countrymen, I do repeat these accusations, and tax them with an utter want of *intellectual* courage—of that higher quality, which is never found without one or other of the three accompaniments, talents, genius,

or principle;—talents matured by the experience, without which it cannot exist at all; or the rapid insight of peculiar genius, by which the fitness of an act may be instantly determined, and which will supply higher motives than mere talents can furnish for encountering difficulty and danger, and will suggest better resources for diminishing or overcoming them. . . . To *consummate* this species of courage, and to render it equal to all occasions . . . *Principle* is indispensibly requisite. I mean that fixed and habitual principle, which implies the absence of all selfish anticipations, whether of hope or fear, and the inward disavowal of any tribunal higher and more dreaded than the mind's own judgment upon its own act. The existence of such principle cannot but elevate the most commanding genius, add rapidity to the quickest glance, a wider range to the most ample comprehension; but, without this principle, the man of ordinary powers must, in the trying hour, be found utterly wanting. Neither, without it, can the man of excelling powers be trust-worthy, or have at all times a calm and confident repose in himself. But he, in whom talents, genius, and principle are united, will have a firm mind, in whatever embarrassment he may be placed; will look steadily at the most undefined shapes of difficulty and danger, of possible mistake or mischance; nor will they appear to him more formidable than they really are. For HIS attention is not distracted—he has but one business, and that is with the object before him. Neither in general conduct nor in particular emergencies, are HIS plans subservient

to considerations of rewards, estate, or title: these
are not to have precedence in his thoughts, to govern
his actions, but to follow in the train of his duty.
(*Cintra*, pp. 55-57)

Instead, the limited abilities of the British commanders
did not even permit them to write an honest and meaningful
proclamation of friendship to their allies; the proclamation that they did write was a mere formula whose language the authors themselves never understood. To General Napier's remark in defense of Wellesley that "a
convention implies some weakness, and must be weighed
in the scales of prudence, not in those of justice,"[9]
Wordsworth would reply that the decisive weakness behind
the Convention of Cintra was mental, not military.

A similar weakness, Wordsworth would say, exists in
critics who have belittled the poet's understanding of
military affairs. He "immensely underrated" the great
importance of clearing the French from Lisbon and all
Portugal, says Dicey.[10] But Wordsworth's war had a
different setting. He saw a struggle not in cities and nations but within the human mind. The aim was to free
minds; to free a city at the cost of the Convention of Cintra
was to mistake "the counters of the game for the stake
played for" (*Cintra*, p. 65). He insisted on a clear distinction between means, like the victory of Vimeiro, and
ends:

The British Generals acted as if they had no purpose

[9] *History of the War in the Peninsula*, 1:164.
[10] Introduction, *Cintra*, p. xix.

but that the enemy should be removed from the country in which they were, upon any terms. Now the
evacuation of Portugal was not the prime object, but
the manner in which that event was to be brought
about; this ought to have been deemed first both in
order and importance;—the French were to be sub-
dued, their ferocious warfare and heinous policy to
be confounded; and in this way, and no other, was the
deliverance of that country to be accomplished. It was
not for soil, or for the cities and forts, that Portugal
was valued, but for the human feeling which was
there; for the rights of human nature which might be
there conspicuously asserted; for a triumph over
injustice and oppression there to be atchieved,
[*sic*], which could neither be concealed nor disguised, and which should penetrate the darkest
corner of the dark Continent of Europe by its
splendour. We combated for victory in the empire
of reason, for strong-holds in the imagination.
(*Cintra*, pp. 64-65)

The war in the Peninsula was, then, a struggle to free
the human imagination and reason, a struggle in which
only strong minds could conquer. What was the point of
the furor caused throughout England by so completely
material a thing as the plunder which the convention permitted the French to carry off? Wordsworth again called
for far-ranging thought. Those people who saw ahead and
saw clearly knew that the plunder was huge but that even
so its size was not of chief concern: "If the value of the
things carried off had been in itself trifling, their grief

and their indignation should have been scarcely less" (*Cintra,* p. 84). The Spanish insurgents who had overwhelmed Dupont at Bailén had set the correct example by depriving the French of all their plunder. This point had been especially emphasized in the extraordinary one-page issue of the *Times* which appeared on the afternoon of August 8, 1808 (see pages 13-14 above). Wordsworth noted how this conduct of the Spaniards was "widely different" from that of the British in Portugal. "With high feeling did they [the Spanish], abating not a jot or a tittle, enforce the principle of justice" (*Cintra,* p. 81). For the British not to have done so was another failure to foresee consequences. Such a failure, Wordsworth realized, would do greater harm to the opponents of the French than a military defeat. Speaking of the effect of the plunder in France when Junot's army arrived there with it, he says:

It is plain that the permission . . . to bear away in triumph the harvest of its crimes, must not only have emboldened and exalted it [the French army] with arrogance, and whetted its rapacity; but that hereby every soldier of which this army was composed, must upon his arrival in his own country, have been a seed which would give back plenteously in its kind. The French are at present a needy people, without commerce or manufactures,—unsettled in their minds and debased in their morals by revolutionary practices and habits of warfare; and the youth of the country are rendered desperate by oppression, which, leaving no choice in their occupation, discharges them from all responsibility to their own consciences.

70

How powerful then must have been the action of such incitements upon a people so circumstanced! The actual sight, and, far more, the imaginary sight and handling of these treasures, magnified by the romantic tales which must have been spread about them, would carry into every town and village an antidote for the terrors of conscription; and would rouze men, like the dreams imported from the new world when the first discoverers and adventurers returned, with their ingots and their gold dust—their stories and their promises, to inflame and madden the avarice of the old. (*Cintra,* pp. 83-84)

One of Wordsworth's principal aims as he began writing the *Cintra* tract was to defend the English public against the charge of prejudging. Following the great outcry which greeted news of the Convention of Cintra, the people of England were finally silenced only by the forceful reprimands of those who supported the generals. One such reprimand, noted by Wordsworth in the tract, which the famous public meeting and petition of the city of London brought forth, was the admonition "that it was inconsistent with the principles of British jurisprudence to pronounce judgement without previous investigation" (*Cintra,* p. 101). The poet responded sharply to this charge of prejudging, which was "re-echoed in its general import by persons who have been over-awed or deceived, and by others who have been wilful deceivers" (*Cintra,* p. 101). Such a charge in such a case seemed to him completely unreasonable. Honest human nature was repelled by the gross immorality of the terms of the convention, and

71

those to blame proclaimed themselves by signing their names to the document:

> If there ever was a case, which could not, in any rational sense of the word, be prejudged, this is one. As to the fact—it appears, and sheds from its own body, like the sun in heaven, the light by which it is seen; as to the person—each has written down with his own hand, *I am the man.* Condemnation of actions and men like these is not, in the minds of a people, (thanks to the divine Being and to human nature!) a matter of choice; it is like a physical necessity, as the hand must be burned which is thrust into the furnace—the body chilled which stands naked in the freezing north-wind. (*Cintra,* pp. 67-68)

If anything was worse than the Convention of Cintra itself, Wordsworth felt, it was this cry of "prejudging," this attempt to defend the convention by cynically invoking the traditions of English legal freedom. He saw clearly that open discussion might most effectively be stifled by a perverse application of the whole basis of British legal rights.

> What need here of a court of judicature to settle who were the persons (their names are subscribed by their own hands), and to determine the quality of the thing? Actions and agents like these, exhibited in this connection with each other, must of necessity be condemned the moment they are known: and to assert the contrary, is to maintain that man is a being

without understanding, and that morality is an empty dream. And, if this condemnation must after this manner follow, to utter it is less a duty than a further inevitable consequence from the constitution of human nature. They, who hold that the formal sanction of a court of judicature is in this case required before a people has a right to pass sentence, know not to what degree they are enemies to that people and to mankind; to what degree selfishness, whether arising from their peculiar situation or from other causes, has in them prevailed over those faculties which are our common inheritance, and cut them off from fellowship with the species. Most deplorable would be the result, if it were possible that the injunctions of these men could be obeyed, or their remonstrances acknowledged to be just. For, (not to mention that, if it were not for such prompt decisions of the public voice, misdemeanours of men high in office would rarely be accounted for at all,) we must bear in mind, at this crisis, that the adversary of all good is hourly and daily extending his ravages; and, according to such notions of fitness, our indignation, our sorrow, our shame, our sense of right and wrong, and all those moral affections, and powers of the understanding, by which alone he can be effectually opposed, are to enter upon a long vacation; their motion is to be suspended—a thing impossible; if it could, it would be destroyed. (*Cintra,* pp. 86-87)

Wordsworth saw greater safety in the public outcry against the convention than in legalisms. In this instance, he heard the voice of the people as infallibly divine.

Not only were the people of England innocent of the charge of prejudging, but those who accused them were themselves guilty of it. The official inquiry was for a time regarded in the popular mind as a demonstration that the Castlereagh government wished to study the facts of the case before expressing a decision publicly. Wordsworth was aware of a general feeling that the court of inquiry would enable the ministry to clear itself from blame for the behavior of the generals. Those who shared this feeling hoped that the inquiry would serve to make the government respectable once more in the eyes of the public. "The people knew what had been their own wishes when the army was sent in aid of their allies; and they clung to the faith, that their wishes and the aims of the Government must have been in unison; and that the guilt would soon be judicially fastened upon those who stood forth as principals, and who (it was hoped) would be found to have fulfilled only their own will and pleasure,—to have had no explicit commission or implied encouragement for what they had done,—no accessaries in their crime" (*Cintra*, p. 98). Those who shared this feeling, who clung to this hope, looked for the government to punish the generals and thereby salvage the nation's honor:

> The punishment of these persons was anticipated, not to satisfy any cravings of vindictive justice (for these, if they could have existed in such a case, had been thoroughly appeased already: for what punishment could be greater than to have brought upon themselves the unremoveable contempt and hatred of

> their countrymen?); but for this reason—that a judicial condemnation of the men, who were openly the proximate cause, and who were forgetfully considered as the single and sole originating source, would make our detestation of the effect more signally manifest. (*Cintra*, p. 98)

Wordsworth, while he recorded this popular hope, had no such illusions. The complicity of the government in the Convention of Cintra was clear to him. The delay in releasing the terms of the convention, the cynical attempt to foment a celebration on the eve of the final appearance of those terms, the "harsh reproof to the City of London" (*Cintra*, p. 101)—this train of events showed that "the spirit which swayed the individuals who were the ostensible and immediate authors of the Convention, was not confined to them" (*Cintra*, p. 99). The official inquiry was, Wordsworth saw, yet another attempt to conceal the fact that the dishonor and mental cowardice of the generals was derived by them from the nation's leaders. The spirit of the convention was strongest among the ruling councils—"there, where if wisdom and virtue have not some influence, what is to become of the nation in these times of peril? rather say, into what an abyss is it already fallen!" (*Cintra*, p. 99)

By the end of 1808, at a time when Wordsworth was still in the early stages of writing the *Cintra* tract, the insurrections on the Peninsula had begun to weaken under the increasing pressure of French troops. Recognizing this "recent calamity," the poet insisted that such tidings, "which too many have received with dismay and despair," should instead lead Englishmen to a deeper and fruitful understanding of both their Spanish allies and their French enemies (*Cintra,* p. 15). Wordsworth wrote to De Quincey in March that English misunderstanding, and worse, misrepresentation, of Spain and Portugal were a primary target of the *Cintra* tract: "One of my principal objects was to refute the calumnies which selfish men had circulated in this country against those two nations."[11] Spain was called by such men a backward and superstitious nation. Many in England accepted Napoleon's claim that the French occupation of the Peninsula would have a fine civilizing and modernizing effect. To this theory "that the *outward* state of the mass of the Spanish people would be improved by the French usurpation," Wordsworth gave "an unqualified denial" (*Cintra,* p. 171). He dealt with the idea imaginatively in the sonnet entitled "Indignation of a High-Minded Spaniard." The poet, who insisted throughout the *Cintra* tract on Englishmen's considering events in the Peninsula from the Spanish viewpoint, assumed that viewpoint himself to attack the claims of Napoleon to be a somewhat disguised blessing for the peoples south of the Pyrenees:

> We can endure that He should waste our lands,
> Despoil our temples, and by sword and flame
> Return us to the dust from which we came;
> Such food a Tyrant's appetite demands:
> And we can brook the thought that by his hands
> Spain may be overpowered, and he possess,
> For his delight, a solemn wilderness

[11] *Letters: Middle Years,* 1:273.

> Where all the brave lie dead. But, when of bands
> Which he will break for us he dares to speak,
> Of benefits, and of a future day
> When our enlightened minds shall bless his sway;
> *Then,* the strained heart of fortitude proves weak;
> Our groans, our blushes, our pale cheeks declare
> That he has power to inflict what we lack strength to
>   bear.[12]

Wordsworth saw the Iberian revolts as the first step in a great purification of the Peninsula—a purification of the kind that Napoleon promised but could not, with his unrighteous means, ever accomplish:

> Spain had risen not merely to be delivered and saved;—deliverance and safety were but intermediate objects;—regeneration and liberty were the end, and the means by which this end was to be attained; had their own high value; were determined and precious; and could no more admit of being departed from, than the end of being forgotten. —She had risen—not merely to be free; but, in the act and process of acquiring that freedom, to recompense herself, as it were in a moment, for all which she had suffered through the ages; to levy, upon the false fame of a cruel Tyrant, large contributions of true glory; to lift herself, by the conflict, as high in honour—as the disgrace was deep to which her own weakness and vices, and the violence and perfidy of her enemies, had subjected her. (*Cintra*, p. 111)

---

[12] *Poetical Works,* 3:137.

Those in England who thought of Spain as backward and superstitious—an unworthy ally—were either blind or dishonest. Either way, Wordsworth wanted to make them see that this mistrusted ally had, in fact, a holy cause. Far from being unworthy, the people of the Peninsula "are instruments of benefit and glory for the human race; and the Deity therefore is with them" (*Cintra,* p. 112). There must be no attempt by England to excuse her own guilt in signing the Convention of Cintra by accusing Spain of ignorance and superstition. The convention was doubly evil for having jeopardized the opportunity for ending that ignorance and that superstition:

> Was there ever—since the earliest actions of men which have been transmitted by affectionate tradition or recorded by faithful history, or sung to the impassioned harp of poetry—was there ever a people who presented themselves to the reason and the imagination, as under more holy influences than the dwellers upon the Southern Peninsula; as rouzed more instantaneously from a deadly sleep to a more hopeful wakefulness . . . ? The superstition (I do not dread the word), which prevailed in these nations, may have checked many of my countrymen who would otherwise have exultingly accompanied me in the challenge which . . . I have been confidently uttering; as I know that this stain (so the same persons termed it) did, from the beginning, discourage their hopes for the cause. Shortsighted despondency! Whatever mixture of superstition there might be in . . . the Spaniards; this must have necessarily been transmuted by that

78

triumphant power, wherever that power was felt, which grows out of intense moral suffering—from the moment in which it coalesces with fervent hope. The chains of bigotry, which enthralled the mind, must have been turned into armour to defend and weapons to annoy. Wherever the heaving and effort of freedom was spread, purification must have followed it. And the types and ancient instruments of error, where emancipated men shewed their foreheads to the day, must have become a language and a ceremony of imagination; expressing, consecrating, and invigorating, the most pure deductions of Reason and the holiest feelings of universal Nature. (*Cintra,* pp. 115-116)

Echoing the English newspapers from which he gathered his information, Wordsworth thrilled to the names of Spanish cities and provinces as if they were holy words. He foresaw the day when "the names of Seville and Andalusia may be consecrated among men, and be words of life to endless generations" (*Cintra,* p. 121).[13] But the poet revealed at the same time his habit, reflected in many of his most famous poems, of distilling the struggle of a people or an era into imaginary character. England had her Michael and her leech-gatherer, and Spain too must have had her solitary peasant hero. Wordsworth's combination of exclaiming over exotic names and imagining isolated and embattled farmers is interesting:

[13] Cf. the exclamatory name-dropping in the *Times* of August 9, and the *Courier* of September 6 and September 16, 1808.

Saragossa!—She also has given bond, by her past actions, that she cannot forget her duty and will not shrink from it. Valencia is under the seal of the same obligation. The multitudes of men who were arrayed in the fields of Baylen, upon the mountains of the North; the peasants of Asturias, and the students of Salamanca; and many a solitary and untold-of hand, which quitting for a moment the plough or the spade, has discharged a more pressing debt to the country by levelling with the dust at least one insolent and murdeous Invader;—these have attested the efficacy of the passions which we have been contemplating— that the will of good men is not a vain impulse, heroic desires a delusive prop. (*Cintra,* p. 121)

It was the failure by England's leaders to imagine the individual patriots in the allied nations, their courage and their problems, which Wordsworth deplored throughout the tract as a prime cause of the feeble spirit of which the Convention of Cintra gave such inescapable evidence. "We may confidently affirm," he wrote in the *Cintra* tract, "that nothing, but a knowledge of human nature directing the operations of our government, can give it a right to an intimate association with a cause which is that of human nature" (*Cintra,* p. 133). Such a knowledge was lacking in the men who ruled England and led her armies. Wordsworth wrote another of his sonnets dedicated to liberty and independence about this lack:

O'erweening Statesmen have full long relied
On fleets and armies, and external wealth:

80

But from *within* proceeds a Nation's health;
Which shall not fail, though poor men cleave with
   pride
To the paternal floor; or turn aside,
In the thronged city, from the walks of gain,
As being all unworthy to detain
A Soul by contemplation sanctified.
There are who cannot languish in this strife,
Spaniards of every rank, by whom the good
Of such high course was felt and understood;
Who to their Country's cause have bound a life
Erewhile, by solemn consecration, given
To labour, and to prayer, to nature, and to heaven.[14]

The *Cintra* tract, the poet hoped, would teach England the lessons and principles by which could be prevented future repetitions of what Winston S. Churchill called "the disgrace of the Convention of Cintra."[15] Wordsworth considered it his primary goal "to be of use in raising and steadying the minds of my countrymen" (*Cintra*, p. 25). It was his faith that "all knowledge of human nature leads ultimately to repose," that is, to the ability to live in hope and honor during "the present or any future struggle which justice will have to maintain against might" (*Cintra*, pp. 25-26).

Dicey is surely correct in admitting as irrelevant the claim made by some critics of the *Cintra* tract that Wordsworth erred in his judgments on the military aspects of the Convention of Cintra.[16] The poet refused ever to

14 *Poetical Works*, 3:138.
15 Churchill, *Age of Revolution*, p. 266.
16 Introduction, *Cintra*, p. xxx.

acknolwedge the supremacy of what are called historical facts. His aim in the tract was not to supply a factual narration of the events which led up to and away from the convention. He sought rather to recall his countrymen to an awareness of recently broken principles, principles based on the acceptance of responsibility, on the sympathetic use of imagination and reason, and on knowledge of human nature. Almost fifteen years later, when he read Southey's more "historical" account of the convention in his friend's *History of the Peninsular War,* Wordsworth reaffirmed the superiority of his own method:

> I have read the whole with great pleasure; the work will do you everlasting honour. I have said the whole, forgetting, in that contemplation, my feelings upon one part, where you have tickled with a feather when you should have branded with a red-hot iron. You will guess I mean the Convention of Cintra. My detestation—I may say abhorrence—of that event is not at all diminished by your account of it. Bonaparte had committed a capital blunder in supposing that when he had intimidated the Sovereigns of Europe he had conquered the several nations. Yet it was natural for a wiser than he to have fallen into this mistake; for the old despotisms had deprived the body of the people of all practical knowledge in the management, and, of necessity, of all interest, in the course of affairs.
>
> The French themselves were astonished at the apathy and ignorance of the people whom they had supposed they had utterly subdued. . . . There was no hope for the deliverance of Europe till the nations

had suffered enough to be driven to a passionate recollection of all that was honourable in their past history and to make appeal to the principles of universal and everlasting justice. These sentiments the authors of that Convention most unfeelingly violated; and as to the principles, they seemed to be as little aware even of the existence of such powers, for powers emphatically may they be called, as the tyrant himself. As far ... as these men could, they put an extinguisher upon the star which was then rising.

It is in vain to say that after the first burst of indignation was over the Portuguese themselves were reconciled to the event, and rejoiced in their deliverance. We may infer from that the horror which they must have felt in the presence of their oppressors; and we may see in it to what a state of helplessness their bad government had reduced them. Our duty was to have treated them with respect, as the representatives of suffering humanity, beyond what they were likely to look for themselves, and as deserving greatly, in common with their Spanish brethren, for having been the first to rise against the tremendous oppression and to show how, and how only, it could be put to an end.[17]

In explaining this difference with Wordsworth, Southey wrote defensively to Henry Crabb Robinson on February 22, 1823, that their mutual friend "is not satisfied with my account of the Con. of Cintra: the rest of the book he

[17] *The Letters of William and Dorothy Wordsworth: The Later Years,* ed. Ernest de Selincourt, 3 vols. (Oxford: Oxford University Press, 1939), 1:167-68 (hereafter cited as *Letters: Later Years*).

likes well. Our difference here is, that he looks at the principle, abstractedly, & I take into view the circumstances."[18] Wordsworth might well have agreed with this explanation. Certainly his whole intent in the *Cintra* tract was to look at principles.

[18] Edith J. Morley, ed., *The Correspondence of Henry Crabb Robinson with the Wordsworth Circle,* 2 vols. (Oxford: Oxford University Press, 1927), 2:125.

4

The Doctrine of National Happiness

Wordsworth described in the *Cintra* tract a system of concentric circles of benevolent relationships by which humanity is surrounded and united. Within the system are the small but important circles of family, friends, party. But "the outermost and all-embracing circle of benevolence" is the nation (*Cintra,* p. 189). All the other relationships "feed and uphold 'the bright consummate flower'—National Happiness—the end, the conspicuous crown, and ornament of the whole" (*Cintra,* p. 190).

If the poet himself attached such importance to it, there might be little wonder that the objective which he called National Happiness has attracted perhaps the greatest attention of commentators on the tract. His thought has been seen as a very significant early manifestation of a doctrine of great importance in the later nineteenth and twentieth centuries: the doctrine of nationalism. For some readers almost the whole importance of the tract lies in its treatment of this doctrine. One such reader finds *Cintra* to be the expression of a shift in "emphasis" from the republicanism of the poet's letter to the bishop of Llandaff and *The Prelude* to a new position of nationalism.[1] Another echoes that in the tract the poet made his appearance as the "champion of nationalism."[2] Re-echoes another reader of the tract: "Its chief interest is in the evidence it furnishes of Wordsworth's change of political principles from republicanism to nationalism."[3] That the doctrine of the tract was prophetic is held by some: "In 1809 Wordsworth had sketched as completely as Mazzini ever did a theory of nationalism that was to become the political faith of the century."[4] And, according to another, "In truth the whole of the *Tract* must be read and re-read in order to perceive how completely he anticipated the enthusiasm for nationality which was fully developed towards the middle of the nineteenth century."[5] Even a critic who says that he does not "share the unreserved admiration which some people have expressed" for the tract agrees with the emphasis of these readers: "Its original contribution to political thought is the doctrine of nationalism."[6]

That this same doctrine held dangers now apparent but of which the author of the *Cintra* tract may not have been fully aware is also noted by some readers. Dicey, in the midst of World War I, asked: "Did Wordsworth . . . in any way foresee results of Nationalism which at the beginning of the twentieth century cause perplexity to thinkers who fully acknowledge the duty and the advantages

[1] James Venable Logan, *Wordsworthian Criticism: A Guide and Bibliography* (Columbus: Ohio State University Press, 1947), pp. 94-95.

[2] Ernest Bernbaum, *Guide through the Romantic Movement* (New York: Ronald Press Co., 1949), p. 85.

[3] Josephine Elizabeth Hildebrandt, "Wordsworth's Prose" (M. A. thesis, Tulane University, 1928), p. 38.

[4] Brinton, *Political Ideas*, p. 58.

[5] Dicey, *Statesmanship of Wordsworth*, p. 80.

[6] Herbert Read, *Wordsworth* (New York: Peter Smith, 1931), p. 236.

of protecting the rights of independent nations?"[7] Dicey finds an answer to his own question: Wordsworth, he says, did indeed fail "to see clearly the peril, which every one now perceives, that the natural and strong sentiment of nationality might degenerate into racial hostility and even into a sort of blood feud, very injurious to the progressive civilization of mankind."[8] Others agree. Herbert Read, noting that Wordsworth's nationalism might be considered a foreshadowing of the theories of Mazzini and Garibaldi, thinks that "in a more chastened mood we may be more inclined to regard him as the prophet of a polity that reached its natural conclusion in the world war of 1914-1918."[9]

The now highly charged term *nationalism,* which Wordsworth himself did not use, could lead an incautious reader today to ascribe too many of the woes of modern times to the kind of thinking which produced the *Cintra* tract. J. C. Smith, for example, writes that Wordsworth did not foresee that the "nationalism" which he preached in the tract would in the twentieth century "spawn its own Napoleons."[10] The same writer seems also to suppose that what so many have spoken of as the nationalism of the tract is a chauvinistic devotion to England—that in the process of opposing Napoleon, Wordsworth's "ardent patriotism had burnt up his cosmopolitanism; from a patriot of the world he had become a patriot of Eng-

[7] Introduction, *Cintra,* p. xxxvii.
[8] Ibid., p. xxxviii.
[9] Read, *Wordsworth,* p. 236.
[10] J.C. Smith, *A Study of Wordsworth,* 2d .ed. rev. (Edinburgh: Oliver & Boyd, 1946), p. 76. The impossibility of such a spawning from Wordsworth's doctrine will be shown throughout the present chapter and in the next.

land."[11]

Clearly it is essential to an understanding of Wordsworth at the time of the composition of the tract to know what he meant by the goal of National Happiness and to see the principles by which he hoped that goal could be attained. It is important first of all to know what the poet meant by the term *nation*. The full title of the *Cintra* tract promises a consideration of the relations which should exist between nations and the preserving or recovering of national freedom and independence. For Wordsworth, nations are not rulers, not governments, not even islands or peninsulas. These things, in fact, may obstruct proper relationships among nations. Nations "are nothing but aggregates of individuals" (*Cintra*, p. 73). A government may deceive itself and may attempt to deceive others that it, and not the people, is the nation. Such deceit was precisely the policy of the English government at the time of the Convention of Cintra. "The people had declared themselves" as emphatically rejecting the convention, and so it was certainly void, in Wordsworth's view. But using as an excuse "the plea of the good faith of the nation being pledged," that is, claiming nationhood for itself, "the ministry took upon itself a final responsibility, with a vain hope that, by so doing and incorporating its own credit with the transaction, it might bear down the censures of the people" (*Cintra,* p. 100).[12] Similarly, military men

[11] Ibid., p. 78. Patriotism there surely was in Wordsworth, but not of a type which excluded interest in other nations. Dicey makes this point when he says that the poet's "English patriotism is so closely united with his faith in the blessing for every country of national independence that in his mind the two sentiments are almost identified with each other"—*Statesmanship of Wordsworth*, p. 83.

[12] A similar distinction between the Portuguese government and the Portuguese nation appears on p. 79 of the tract and between the Spanish nation and

may think of a nation as being summed up in its military power. But such thinking confuses the whole with the parts. In the struggle to recover Spanish national independence from the French, wrote Wordsworth, "the true army of Spain . . . is the whole people" (*Cintra,* p. 182). And again, "The whole Spanish nation ought to be encouraged to deem themselves an army, embodied under the authority of their country and of human nature" (*Cintra,* p. 20). It was typical of the British generals who agreed to the Convention of Cintra that they discounted or perhaps knew nothing of the strength of nations in Wordsworth's sense of the word. These generals overlooked even the military problems for the French commander of having to rule a "people . . . detesting him, and stung almost to madness" (*Cintra,* p. 55). The poet cited with approval one of the Spanish proclamations of the insurrection: "A whole people is more powerful than disciplined armies" (*Cintra,* p. 41). The generals and ministers of England, however, accepted the French position that the people of occupied Spain and Portugal were only peasants in revolt (*Cintra,* p. 19). For Wordsworth, these people *were* Spain and Portugal, a fact in which lay great military strength: "Was the hatred and abhorrence of the Portugueze and Spanish Nations nothing?" (*Cintra,* p. 55) This same point was made memorably in a sonnet composed in 1811:

The power of Armies is a visible thing,

government on pp. 11-12. This distinction is by no means original with Wordsworth. But it was still new enough that a year before it had seemed quite revolutionary when it had formed the basis of Foreign Minister George Canning's policy following the original Spanish uprisings against Napoleon. See Rose, *Nationality in Modern History,* p. 62.

Formal, and circumscribed in time and space;
But who the limits of that power shall trace
Which a brave People into light can bring
Or hide, at will,—for freedom combating
By just revenge inflamed? No foot may chase,
No eye can follow, to a fatal place
That power, that spirit, whether on the wing
Like the strong wind, or sleeping like the wind
Within its awful caves.—From year to year
Springs this indigenous produce far and near;
No craft this subtle element can bind,
Rising like water from the soil, to find
In every nook a lip that it may cheer.[13]

It is essential to an understanding of everything which Wordsworth had to say about National Happiness to keep clearly in mind the fact that he used the word *nation* to mean the people of a country—"a People, which has lived long, feels that it has a Country to love; and where the heart of the People is sound" (*Cintra,* p. 158).

Despite the failure of England's rulers to grasp the truth, Wordsworth's own faith that the people constitute the essence of a nation was immensely strengthened by the peninsular revolts. A nation which in fact is the creation as well as the aggregate of the people is also the noble product of nature and civilization acting in concert; in explaining this idea Wordsworth showed more fully what he meant by considering a nation as a people:

The events of the last year, gloriously destroying

[13] *Poetical Works,* 3:139-140.

many frail fears, have placed—in the rank of serene
and immortal truths—a proposition which, as an object
of belief, hath in all ages been fondly cherished;
namely—That a numerous Nation, determined to be
free, may effect its purpose in despite of the mightiest
power which a foreign Invader can bring against it.
These events also have pointed out how, in the ways
of Nature and under the guidance of Society, this
happy end is to be attained: in other words, they have
shewn that the cause of the People, in dangers and
difficulties issuing from this quarter of oppression,
is safe while it remains not only in the bosom but in
the hands of the People; or (what amounts to the same
thing) in those of a government which, being truly
from the People, is faithfully *for* them. (*Cintra,*
pp. 155-156)

The Convention of Cintra was, by contrast, the unholy
product of cynicism in high places in England coupled
with ignorance of this process by which nations are
created and composed. The poet saw the convention and
the official actions which followed it and attempted to
cloak it as unfortunately not isolated incidents in his
country's history. The recent history of England, in fact,
was already besmirched by the same callous approach to
the rights of nations, in Wordsworth's sense of the word
nation, as had been exhibited in the generals' treatment
of the Spanish and the Portuguese: "In the course of the
last thirty years we have seen two wars waged against
Liberty—the American war, and the war against the French
People in the early stages of their Revolution. . . . And

... at this time, we may affirm—that the same presumptuous
irreverence of the principles of justice, and blank insensibility to the affections of human nature, which determined the conduct of our government in those two wars
against liberty, have continued to accompany its exertions in the present struggle *for* liberty,—and have rendered them fruitless." Furthermore, Wordsworth added,
excuses based on self-deception are not valid: "The British government deems ... that its intentions are good. It
must not deceive itself: nor must we deceive ourselves.
Intentions—thoroughly good—could not mingle with the un-
blessed actions which we have witnessed. A disinterested
and pure intention is a light that guides as well as cheers,
and renders, desperate lapses impossible" (*Cintra*, pp.
140-141).

Wordsworth was obviously no chauvinist. His sights,
rather, were always on the responsibility of the English
nation—a responsibility generally met by the nation, the
people, but dishonorably evaded by the generals and the
government. The English nation had a great opportunity
at the time of the insurrections in the Peninsula. But the
blame for losing the opportunity did not belong to the nation: "Then it was that we—not we, but the heads of the
British army and nation— ... stepped in with their forms,
their impediments, their rotten customs and precedents,
their narrow desires, their busy and purblind fears"
(*Cintra*, p. 127). Here Wordsworth clearly saw the distinction between the nation and the nation's heads. But he
feared that the Spanish and Portuguese might not, in
their immense dismay over the Convention of Cintra, be
able to make such distinctions:

Independence and liberty were the blessings for which the people of the Peninsula were contending—immediate independence, which was not to be gained but by modes of exertion from which liberty must ensue. Now, liberty—healthy, matured, time-honoured liberty—this is the growth and peculiar boast of Britain; and nature herself, by encircling with the ocean the country which we inhabit, has proclaimed that this mighty nation is for ever to be her own ruler, and that the land is set apart for the home of immortal independence. Judging then from these first fruits of British Friendship, what bewildering and depressing and hollow thoughts must the Spaniards and Portugueze have entertained concerning the real value of these blessings, if the people who have possessed them longest, and who ought to understand them best, could send forth an army capable of enacting the oppression and baseness of the Convention of Cintra; if the government of that people could sanction this treaty; and if, lastly, this distinguished and favoured people themselves could suffer it to be held forth to the eyes of men as expressing the sense of their hearts—as an image of their understandings. (*Cintra,* p. 96)

It is consistent with his idea of what constitutes a nation that Wordsworth would stand up for his people while attacking their military and government leaders. And against the natural and likely confusion of the peninsular peoples, he defended his fellow Englishmen, his nation. The defense, however, would hardly appeal to the kind of

English nationalist which some have accused the poet himself of being. Of the reaction of the English nation to the convention, he wrote: "It did not speak their sense—it was not endured—it was not submitted to in their hearts. Bitter was the sorrow of the people of Great Britain ... —overwhelming was their astonishment, tormenting their shame; their indignation was tumultuous" (*Cintra,* p. 96). Such a defense is not chauvinism. It hardly permits the interpretation that Wordsworth was driven by his hatred of Napoleon into expressing in the tract a belief that England was "ideal as it was."[14] But Wordsworth's argument on behalf of his countrymen did permit Coleridge to make a significant comparison when he called the *Cintra* tract "the grandest politico-moral work since Milton's De-fensio Pop. Anglic.,"[15] for both works insisted on the distinction between the rulers who may try to corrupt a nation and the people who, because they actually constitute the nation, have the right to oppose their rulers to halt the corruption. The goal of National Happiness hoped for in the *Cintra* tract, then, does not mean the exaltation of England and English policy. It necessitates rather a very significant definition of what for Wordsworth consti-tuted a nation, and a reminder that although the English generals and government can be depraved the English people must retain their sense of duty.

The goal of National Happiness, Wordsworth believed, was to be achieved by using together as in a single process four essential methods.[16] All four of these methods are

[14] George Brandes, *Main Currents in Nineteenth Century Literature,* vol. 4, *Naturalism in England* (New York: Boni & Liveright, 1905), p. 86.

[15] Griggs, *Letters of Coleridge,* 3:273.

[16] Dicey finds five principles "which sum up the statesmanship of Words-worth": first, national independence is essential to civil liberty; second, every

explicit in the *Cintra* tract, and Wordsworth treated them also in his letter to Captain Charles William Pasley of the Royal Engineers, a letter which the poet seems to have considered a kind of supplement to the tract. In the following discussion of the means by which National Happiness could be found, the tract and the letter will be considered together.

One of the methods which Wordsworth considered essential to achieving National Happiness is awareness of and adherence to the principle that the independence of a people, a nation, is necessary for human progress. By national independence the poet meant that a people lived under a government of whatever form but of its own choosing; thus, France under Napoleon was no more independent in this sense than Spain under Napoleon. Lacking this independence, neither nation (nor any other in such circumstances) could achieve genuine and lasting progress. "Was there ever an instance, since the world began, of the peaceful arts thriving under a despotism so oppressive as that of France is and must continue to be?"[17] Wordsworth supplied his own answer: "Whatever may be

---

independent nation is interested in the maintenance of the independence of every other country; third, no state should possess such power as to menace another's independence; fourth, the French under Napoleon possess such dangerous power, and it must be broken; fifth, a new balance of power in Europe is desirable, one based on linguistic boundaries. See *Statesmanship of Wordsworth,* pp. 76, 86-93. Any student of the *Cintra* tract must acknowledge his debt to Dicey's work, as do I, particularly for the general theme and organization of the following discussion, even while recognizing that in the presentation of Wordsworth's "doctrines of nationalism," as indeed throughout his book, there is a tendency, understandable in one writing in the midst of World War I, for Dicey to neglect Wordsworth's immediate concern over Napoleon and the Peninsula in 1809 and see the tract largely as a timely reminder to Englishmen in the struggle with the Kaiser of their patriotic duty and heritage.

[17] *Letters: Middle Years,* 1:432.

the form of a government, its spirit, at least, must be mild and free before agriculture, trade, commerce, and manufactures can thrive under it; and if these do not prosper in a State, it may extend its empire to right and to left, and it will only carry poverty and desolation along with it, without being itself permanently enriched."[18] It was this principle which made the struggle for Spanish and Portuguese independence of such immense importance in the poet's thinking. And it was this same principle which the rulers and generals of England ignored and the potential benefits of which their conduct jeopardized. The poet wrote:

> I will now beg of my reader to pause a moment and to review in his own mind the whole of what has been laid before him. He has seen of what kind, and how great have been the injuries endured by these two nations; what they have suffered, and what they have to fear; he has seen that they have felt with that unanimity which nothing but the light of truth spread over the inmost concerns of human nature can create; with that simultaneousness which has led Philosophers upon like occasions to assert, that the voice of the people is the voice of God. He has seen that they have submitted as far as human nature could bear; and that at last these millions ... have risen almost like one man, with one hope; for whether they look to triumph or defeat, to victory or death, they are full of hope—despair comes not near them—they will die, they say—each individual knows the danger, and

[18] Ibid., p. 433.

strong in the magnitude of it, grasps eagerly at the thought that he himself is to perish; and more eagerly, and with higher confidence, does he lay to his heart the faith that the nation will survive and be victorious; —or, at the worst, let the contest terminate how it may as to superiority of outward strength, that the fortitude and the martyrdom, the justice and the blessing, are their's and cannot be relinquished. And not only are they moved by these exalted sentiments of universal morality and of direct and universal concern to mankind, which have impelled them to resist evil and to endeavour to punish the evil-doer, but also they descend . . . to express a rational hope of reforming domestic abuses, and of re-constructing . . . a better frame of civil government, the same in the great outlines of its architecture, but exhibiting the knowledge, and genius, and the needs of the present race, harmoniously blended with those of their forefathers. Woe, then, to the unworthy who intrude with their help to maintain this most sacred cause! (*Cintra,* pp. 41-43)

The English nation knew what the English leaders did not, that the real goal in the Peninsula was not just to defeat Napoleon nor to force the French to evacuate the conquered lands. The principal immediate objective, of necessity intertwined with the other two, was the building of a government which would allow and encourage human progress: "The first end to be secured . . . is riddance of the enemy: the second, permanent independence: and the third, a free constitution of government; which will

97

give their main (though far from sole) value to the other two" (*Cintra*, p. 162). These ends must all be achieved together; without the third one, the one overlooked by England's leaders, "little more than a formal independence, and perhaps scarcely that, can be secured" (*Cintra,* p. 162).

Also required for National Happiness is sincere acceptance of the principle that the genuine independence of a people depends on the virtue and devotion to justice of that people. Much of Napoleon's early success, it seemed to Wordsworth, lay in the fact that the nations which he conquered were not virtuous. When such a nation fell to the conqueror—the examples cited in the tract are Prussia and Austria—the poet felt no fervor for the defeated: "A nation, without the virtues necessary for the attainment of independence, have failed to attain it. This is all" (*Cintra,* p. 25). But the rising against tyranny of whole peoples in the Peninsula proved that the nations there were of a different type: "Little has that man understood the majesty of true national freedom, who believes that a population like that of Spain, may want the qualities needful to fight out their independence, and yet possess the excellencies which render men susceptible of true liberty" (*Cintra*, p. 25). This principle, too, had been ignored by those who wrote and accepted the Convention of Cintra. As Wordsworth wrote to Southey: "There was no hope for the deliverance of Europe till the nations had suffered enough to be driven to a passionate recollection of all that was honourable in their past history and to make appeal to the principles of universal and everlasting justice." The hope arose in the Peninsula, but "these

98

sentiments the authors of that Convention most unfeelingly violated."[19] Again the generals' problem was a confusion of objectives. Having no sight of righteous goals, they were not concerned with righteous methods. Wordsworth called for a moral perspective: "Our duty is—our aim ought to be—to employ the true means of liberty and virtue for the ends of liberty and virtue. In such policy, thoroughly understood, there is fitness and concord and rational subordination" (*Cintra*, p. 141). Agreeing with Captain Pasley that military power was essential to the goal of a free Europe composed of independent nations, Wordsworth nevertheless put national virtue first: "I . . . rest my hopes with respect to the emancipation of Europe more upon moral influence, and the wishes and opinions of the people of the respective nations, than you appear to do. As I have written in my pamphlet, 'on the moral qualities of a people must its salvation untimately depend. Something higher than military excellence must be taught *as* higher; something more fundamental, *as* more fundamental.' "[20]

In her excellent study of Wordsworth's debt to Roman political writers, Jane Worthington states her belief that when "Wordsworth entrusted both national and international welfare to a principle of virtue,"[21] he had certain specific virtues in mind. These, she says, were "the old domestic morals of the land" listed in book 8 of *The Excursion* (lines 239-42):

> The character of peace,
> Sobriety, and order, and chaste love,

19 Ibid., p. 167.
20 Ibid., p. 436.
21 Worthington, *Wordsworth's Reading of Roman Prose*, p. 31.

And honest dealing, and untainted speech,
And pure good-will, and hospitable cheer.[22]

If specific virtues must be cited, however, upon which Wordsworth's goal of national independence was to be built, they may more likely be those he listed in the tract itself as being possessed by the people of the Peninsula:

> Moral qualities of a high order, and vehement passions, and virtuous as vehement, the Spanish have already displayed.... Their strength *chiefly* lies in moral qualities, more silent in their operation, more permanent in their nature; in the virtues of perseverance, constancy, fortitude, and watchfulness, in a long memory and a quick feeling, to rise upon a favourable summons, a texture of life which, though cut through (as hath been feigned of the bodies of the Angels) unites again—these are the virtues and qualities on which the Spanish People must be taught *mainly* to depend. (*Cintra*, p. 22; italics in original)

Clearly, however, the poet intended no such limitation on essential national virtue as any list would imply. He seems rather to have felt that the degree of true independence which a people could achieve would correspond to the degree of virtue it possessed. The possibilities were unlimited, and so were the responsibilities: "When wickedness acknowledges no limit but the extent of her power, and advances with aggravated impatience like a devouring fire; the only worthy or adequate opposition is—that of

---

[22] *Poetical Works,* 5:273.

virtue submitting to no circumscription of her endeavors save that of her rights, and aspiring from the impulse of her own ethereal zeal. The Christian exhortation for the individual is here the precept for nations—'Be ye therefore perfect; even as your Father, which is in Heaven, is perfect' " (*Cintra*, pp. 188-89).

Another way by which Wordsworth's objective of National Happiness is attained is by acting upon the knowledge that each nation preserves its own independence by defending that of other nations. The poet was very favorably impressed by the proclamation of the Spanish insurrectionists, issued at Oviedo on July 17, 1808, which he quoted in the tract: "Spain will inevitably conquer, in a cause the most just that has ever raised the deadly weapon of war; for she fights, not for the concerns of a day, but for the security and happiness of ages; not for an insulated privilege, but for the rights of human nature; not for temporal blessings, but for eternal happiness; not for the benefit of one nation, but for all mankind, and even for France herself" (*Cintra,* p. 41). Here again the government and generals of England violated, by the Convention of Cintra, a principle from which their own nation could otherwise have benefited as much as the peninsular allies. These men understood so little the true nature of the alliance between the peoples of England, Portugal, and Spain that they despised the people they ought to have trusted and failed to see that "their liberty, independence, and honour, are our genuine gain" (*Cintra*, p. 133). Wordsworth felt keenly the need in England for "a General and a Ministry whose policy would be comprehensive enough to perceive that the true welfare of Britain is best promoted by the independence, freedom, and honour of other Nations" (*Cintra,* p. 150). Instead, the leaders of England could only attempt to excuse themselves by accusing their allies of being untrustworthy.[23] Wordsworth believed that the strength of England's own independence—the strength of the English people's freedom of choice—depended finally on the independence of peoples like the Portuguese and Spanish. He called, therefore, for a treatment of such allies exactly opposite to that which they had received from English leaders:

> We ought to have endeavoured to raise the Portugueze in their own estimation by concealing our power in comparison with theirs; dealing with them in the spirit of those mild and humane delusions, which spread such a genial grace over the intercourse, and add so much to the influence of love in the concerns of private life. It is a common saying, presume that a man is dishonest, and that is the readiest way to make him so: in like manner it may be said, presume that a nation is weak, and that is the surest course to bring it to weakness,—if it be not rouzed to prove its strength by applying it to the humiliation of your pride. The Portugueze had been weak; and, in connection with their allies the Spaniards, they were prepared to become strong. It was, therefore, doubly incumbent upon us to foster and encourage them—to look favourably upon their efforts—generously to give them credit upon their promises—to hope with them and for them; and, thus anticipating and foreseeing,

[23] General Napier's comment is an example; see p. 59 above.

102

we should, by a natural operation of love, have contributed to create the merits which were anticipated
and foreseen. (*Cintra,* p. 73)

All English military intervention in nations occupied by
Napoleon, Wordsworth insisted to Captain Pasley, ought
to be "not for our sakes directly, but for the benefit of
those unhappy nations whom we should rescue, and whose
prosperity would be reflected back upon ourselves."[24]
Failure to understand the truth and importance of this
principle of the interdependence of independent nations
was extremely dangerous, according to the poet. Such
failure would destroy the integrity of whole nations and
of individuals. Wordsworth loved England despite her
many failings, and he hoped his words might penetrate the
English consciousness in time to save his nation:

It is to the worldlings of our own country, and to
those who think without carrying their thoughts far
enough, that I address myself. Let them know, there
is no true wisdom without imagination; no genuine
sense;—that the man, who in this age feels no regret
for the ruined honour of other Nations, must be poor
in sympathy for the honour of his own Country; and
that, if he be wanting here towards that which circum-
scribes the whole, he neither has—nor can have—a
social regard for the lesser communities which
Country includes. Contract the circle, and bring him
to his family; such a man cannot protect *that* with
dignified loves. Reduce his thoughts to his own per-

[24] *Letters: Middle Years,* 1:436.

son; he may defend himself,—what *he* deems his honour; but it is the *action* of a brave man from the impulse of the brute, or the motive of a coward. (*Cintra,* p. 171)

A final step in the process by which Wordsworth believed that National Happiness would be achieved was through a new and durable kind of balance of power among European nations. Important to the attainment of this goal is the recognition that the truly internal affairs of a nation are its own concern and that what the poet thought of as real independence grants a people the right to choose any form of government for itself. Thus a nation might be independent and yet not free. Wordsworth, of course championing freedom, still held that independence even without internal freedom brought important blessings:

The difference, between inbred oppression and that which is from without, is *essential;* inasmuch as the former does not exclude from the minds of a people, the feeling of being self-governed; does not imply (as the latter does, when patiently submitted to) an abandonment of the first duty imposed by the faculty of reason. . . . If a country have put on chains of its own forging; in the name of virtue, let it be conscious that to itself it is accountable: let it not have cause to look beyond its own limits for reproof: and,—in the name of humanity—if it be self-depressed, let it have its pride and some hope within itself. (*Cintra,* pp. 167-69)

Wordsworth claimed too that this respect by other nations

for the internal affairs of a people could operate so as to allow, with the approval of the inhabitants, the uniting of "contiguous or neighbouring countries, both included by nature under one conspicuously defined limit" (*Cintra* p. 163).

To achieve the balance of power which he visualized, Wordsworth warned that no nation should be possessed of irresistible power. The evil effects of such power were to be seen "in the tyranny which the French Nation maintains over Europe"—of which the French people were also victims (*Cintra,* p. 145). But when Captain Pasley suggested that English armies ought to destroy the French tyranny by driving out Napoleon's troops and occupying the Continent themselves, Wordsworth replied: "I do not think that so wide a space of conquered country is desirable; and as a Patriot I have no wish for it."[25] The consequences to England would be as disruptive of human progress as Napoleon's empire-building in Europe had been for France. Wordsworth hoped England would instead avoid the dangers which he felt inevitably accompanied too much power:

> Woe be to that country whose military power is irresistible! I deprecate such an event for Great Britain scarcely less than for any other land. Scipio foresaw the evils with which Rome would be visited when no Carthage should be in existence for her to contend with. If a nation have nothing to oppose or to fear without, it cannot escape decay and concussion within. Universal triumph and absolute security soon

[25] Ibid.

105

betray a State into abandonment of that discipline, civil and military, by which its victories were secured. If the time should ever come when this Island shall have no more formidable enemies by land than it has at this moment by sea, the extinction of all that it previously contained of good and great would soon follow. Indefinite progress, undoubtedly, there ought to be somewhere; but let that be in knowledge, in science, in civilization, in the increase of the numbers of the people, and in the augmentation of their virtue and happiness; but progress in conquest cannot be indefinite; and for that very reason, if for no other, it cannot be a fit object for the exertions of a people, I mean beyond certain limits, which, of course, will vary with circumstances. My prayer, as a Patriot, is, that we may always have, somewhere or other, enemies capable of resisting us, and keeping us at arm's length.[26]

The final step required for the new European equilibrium envisioned by Wordsworth was a continuation in modern times of the historical process of the uniting of small states too weak to defend themselves into a few strong nations. Such unions were acceptable uses of the internal powers of independent states. One such union had occurred, with some unpleasantness but yet successfully, so Wordsworth believed, in the British Isles. "Who does

[26] Ibid., p. 438. Dicey's apparently paradoxical comment that Wordsworth revealed in the sonnets on liberty that he took comfort in the "assurance of England's irresistible strength" as a defender of the freedom of nations seems rather to imply a distinction (by Dicey, if not Wordsworth) between the irresistibility of a moral cause and the admittedly pernicious effects of "irresistible military power." See *Statesmanship of Wordsworth*, pp. 79,89.

not rejoice that former partitions have disappeared,—and that England, Scotland, and Wales are under one legislative and executive authority; and that Ireland (would that she had been more justly dealt with!) follows the same destiny?" (*Cintra,* pp. 163-64). Nor did the poet connect the modern tyranny of Napoleon with the rightful creation in past centuries of the French state out of "the large and numerous Fiefs, which interfered injuriously with the grand demarcation assigned by nature to France" (*Cintra,* p. 164). He hoped that Spain might eventually achieve "a free union with Portugal" because their traditions, their spirit, and their geography "point out and command that the two nations of the Peninsula should be united in friendship and strict alliance; and, as soon as it may be effected without injustice, form one independent and indissoluble sovereignty" (*Cintra,* p. 164). Looking ahead half a century, Wordsworth predicted the unification of Italy and of Germany: "The several independent Sovereignties of Italy (a country, the boundary of which is still more expressly traced out by nature; and which has no less the further definition and cement of country which Language prepares) have yet this good to aim at: and it will be a happy day for Europe, when the natives of Italy and the natives of Germany (whose duty is, in like manner, indicated to them) shall each dissolve the pernicious barriers which divide them, and form themselves into a mighty People" (*Cintra,* p. 164).[27] The free and peaceful Europe

[27] Much has been made of this prophecy (see p. 86 above), but Wordsworth seems not to have thought of these words as a long-range prediction. His remarks on p. 190 of *Cintra* indicate that he hoped for the German and Italian unifications to be accomplished in time to help overthrow Napoleon. To Pasley he wrote: "I think there is nothing more unfortunate for Europe than the condition of Germany and Italy in these respects; could the barriers

envisioned by the poet could more easily arise in his day
than in earlier ages. Napoleon had, by his destruction of
so many corrupt regimes, unwittingly prepared the way.
In the post-Napoleonic era, statesmen would have unparalleled opportunity to build a better world. In the place of
the emperor's tyranny could stand, by the wise efforts of
visionary statesmen, six great states, balanced in power
and influence. Smaller states might freely unite with
these, as Wordsworth had already explained in the case of
the Peninsula. He had little faith, as the next chapter will
show, in statesmen; but he hoped for divine intervention,
and he prayed. To Pasley he wrote:

> Such is the present condition of Europe, that I ear-
> nestly pray for what I deem would be a mighty
> blessing. France has already destroyed, in almost
> every part of the Continent, the detestable Govern-
> ments with which the nations have been afflicted;
> she has extinguished one sort of tyranny, but only to
> substitute another. Thus, then, have the countries of
> Europe been taught, that domestic oppression, if not
> manfully and zealously repelled, must sooner or
> later be succeeded by subjugation from without; they
> have tasted the bitterness of both cups, have drunk
> deeply of both. Their spirits are prepared for re-
> sistance to the foreign Tyrant, and with our help I
> think they may shake him off, and, under our coun-
> tenance, and following (as far as they are capable)

be dissolved which have divided the one nation into Neapolitans, Tuscans,
Venetians, &c., and the other into Prussians, Hanoverians, &c., and could they
once be taught to feel their strength, the French would be driven back into
their own land immediately" *(Letters: Middle Years*, 1:438).

our example, they may fashion to themselves, making use of what is best in their own ancient laws and institutions, new forms of government, which may secure posterity from a repetition of such calamities as the present age has brought forth. The materials of a new balance of power exist in the language, and name, and territory of Spain, in those of France, and those of Italy, Germany, Russia, and the British Isles. The smaller States must disappear, and merge in the large nations and wide-spread languages. The possibility of this remodelling of Europe I see clearly; earnestly do I pray for it.[28]

Wordsworth's objective of National Happiness was far from being vainglorious patriotism or nationalism. The poet's eyes were on more enduring and trustworthy things than the trappings of governments or boundaries or military power which have come to be called nationalist. His aims were high, and he had no delusions about the difficulties. But the new Europe he envisioned seemed well worth the trouble. Captain Pasley wrote that England needed a new military policy to meet the challenges of the day. Replied Wordsworth: "England, as well as the rest of Europe, requires what is more difficult to give it,—a new course of education." Only in this way could be instilled "a higher tone of moral feeling, more of the grandeur of the Imaginative faculties, and less of the petty processes of the unfeeling and purblind understanding, that would manage the concerns of nations in the same calculating spirit with which it would set about building a

[28] *Letters: Middle Years.* 1:439.

house." [29] National Happiness was for Wordsworth a moral objective requiring men's highest faculties and truly moral means to be achieved.

[29] Ibid., p. 440.

5
Poet and People, Statesmen and Generals, and the Doctrine of Leadership

In the *Cintra* tract, according to Samuel Chew, "Wordsworth enunciated an anti-democratic doctrine of leadership which foreshadows the 'hero-worship' of Carlyle."[1] Claiming to have found the same doctrine in the tract, B. H. Lehman calls it "a conservative . . . idea of great men" and gives it as the reason for the tract's being lifted in his opinion "upon the Miltonic plane."[2] Just exactly what Carlyle himself meant by "heroes" and "hero worship" of course remains a matter of interpretation and even some controversy. More to the point than what Carlyle meant, however, is what he has been interpreted as meaning by those who find his teachings foreshadowed in Wordsworth. The same B. H. Lehman, in his study of Carlyle's theory of the hero, in which he cites Wordsworth's tract as an influence on that theory, arrives at an essential definition of the great man which needs to be compared with Wordsworth's thoughts. The great man, according to Lehman's reading of Carlyle, is one who has

[1] Albert C. Baugh, ed., *A Literary History of England*, vol. 4, Samuel C. Chew, *The Nineteenth Century and After* (New York: Appleton-Century-Crofts, 1948), p. 1145.
[2] B. H. Lehman, "The Doctrine of Leadership in the Greater Romantic Poets," *PMLA* 31 (1922): 640.

an original insight into the true reality of life and a disbelief in semblances.[3] Further, the great man is completely though perhaps unconsciously sincere; he is, in short, "a being gifted with understanding and foresight and with ability to make good his excellent intention." The hero of this theory, famous in association with Carlyle, includes Wordsworth in his ancestry, says Lehman: "Wordsworth's conception of a great man is implicit in all but his very earliest writing. It is explicit and even elaborated in the great [*Cintra*] tract." The basic concept of the hero, common to both Carlyle and Wordsworth, Lehman says, includes those qualities of leadership which the poet claimed in the tract as governing "the actions of heroes, statesmen, legislators, and warriors."[4]

The poet who, in 1793, had dismissed "titles, ... stars, ribbons, and garters" as "badges of fictitious superiority" was hardly a believer in Carlyle's heroes at that time. In his letter to Bishop Watson of Llandaff that year, Wordsworth had looked upon those in whom the bishop, a true hero-worshipper, placed his faith as "depraved" in their principles and "contemptible" in their understandings. This early Wordsworth saw only danger and trouble arising from heroes and hero worship. "What services," he asked, "can a man render to society to compensate for the outrage done to the dignity of our nature when we bind ourselves to address him and his posterity with humiliating circumlocutions, calling him

---

[3] B. H. Lehman, *Carlyle's Theory of the Hero: Its Sources, Development, History, and Influence on Carlyle's Work* (Durham: Duke University Press, 1928), pp. 47, 54. Lehman admits (p. 138) that regarding Carlyle's debt to Wordsworth, "I am arguing for an unconscious influence at most."

[4] Ibid., pp. 48-50, 137, 139, 140.

most noble, most honourable, most high, most august, serene, excellent, eminent, and so forth?" The danger was as great for the prospective hero: "Such unnatural flattery will but generate vices which ought to consign him to neglect and solitude, or make him the perpetual object of the finger of scorn." And yet Wordsworth recognized that, for all the dangers, men claiming to be heroes can often impose their claims: "Alas, the world is weak enough to grant the indulgence which they assume."[5] Everywhere in the letter to Bishop Watson, the poet was at pains to discredit the kind of leadership theory which Chew and Lehman find him championing in the *Cintra* tract fifteen years later. The elevation of men into "great men," he believed, destines them for the kind of catastrophe which overtook Louis XVI. Such elevation—whether it comes by the inheritance of high rank and power or by popular acclaim, obedience, and even reverence for real or supposed superiority—such elevation always denies a man the kind of experience and education which leads to the understanding and knowledge essential to Lehman's definition. The trouble begins, according to Wordsworth, when "the prejudice and weakness of mankind have made it necessary to force an individual into an unnatural situation, which requires more than human talents and human virtues, and at the same time precludes him from attaining even a moderate knowledge of human life, and from feeling a particular share in the interests of mankind."[6]

[5] "Apology for the French Revolution, 1793," in *The Prose Works of William Wordsworth*, ed. Alexander B. Grosart, 3 vols. (London: E. Moxon, Son, ard Co., 1876), 1:17.
[6] Ibid., p. 5.

If the author of the letter to Bishop Watson of 1793 became, in the *Cintra* tract of 1809, a preacher of an "anti-democratic doctrine of leadership," as Chew says, the change was a fundamental and important one. Thus, the claims of Chew and Lehman demand an examination of the tract itself.

The times of the peninsular uprisings and the Convention of Cintra may have had their heroes. Napoleon himself seemed to some to be the great man, as Wellington did to others. Against the tendency of some Englishmen to elevate Wellesley and his companions to the role of hero, influential voices were raised in Wordsworth's day. Leigh Hunt wrote in the *Examiner* that while Wellesley was receiving titles and accolades at home, "abroad he led a corrupted army for the benefit of corrupt and corrupting monarchs."[7] Sir Walter Scott called the convention which followed the victory of the allied forces over the French at Vimeiro "one of those numerous instances, in which the soldiers gain the battle from confidence in their own hearts, and the general fails to improve it, perhaps from an equally just diffidence of his own skill and talents."[8] From the Peninsula came ironic words which could not strengthen faith in England's leaders. General John Moore, who succeeded to the command of English troops there when the other generals were recalled to London following the Convention of Cintra, wrote Parliament: "The [Spanish revolutionary] government are resolute, and every man of them determined to perish with the country: they will not, at least, set the example which the ruling powers and higher orders of

[7] Houtchens and Houtchens, *Leigh Hunt's Essays*, p. 56.
[8] Scott, *Life of Napoleon*, 2:34.

114

other countries have exhibited, of weakness and timid-
ity."[9] As the following consideration of the treatment
given leaders and hero-worshippers in the *Cintra* tract
will show, Wordsworth's views on the subject actually
were not anticipatory of Carlyle's doctrine of leadership
at all but were instead part of the widespread alarm and
indignation over such theories in which Hunt, Scott, and
Moore also had a share.

It is true that Wordsworth had written in the 1805
version of *The Prelude* of "ancient Heroes" and had
declared:

> There is
> One great Society alone on earth,
> The noble Living and the noble Dead.[10]

It is true that in the same year that the *Cintra* tract
appeared, Wordsworth wrote and published a sonnet on
Andrew Hofer, the innkeeper who led the Tyrolese in
their fight aginst the French, in which the poet called
Hofer "the Hero" and seemed to wonder whether the
Austrian had mortal parents or was a reincarnation of
the great William Tell.[11] And it is true that in the *Cintra*
tract itself Wordsworth wrote of heroes of both the dis-
tant and the recent past, and wrote in the same context
of the value of heeding "the glorious example of . . .

[9] James Moore, *A Narrative of the Campaign of the British Army in Spain* (London, 1809), p. 82.
[10] *The Prelude, or Growth of a Poet's Mind*, ed. Ernest de Selincourt, 2d ed. rev. Helen Darbishire (Oxford: Oxford University Press, 1959), p. 422 (bk. 10, lines 955, 968-70); hereafter cited as *Prelude*. The language is retained in the 1850 *Prelude*, p. 423 (bk. 11, lines 383, 393-95).
[11] *Poetical Works*, 3:129.

worthy progenitors" (*Cintra,* p. 37). Numerous references like these to what at first glance might look like a Carlylesque doctrine of heroes and hero worship have perhaps contributed to the misunderstanding of the poet's true teaching.

Wordsworth had, indeed, a great deal to say in the tract about leaders and would-be heroes; nowhere in the scene which he surveyed, however, did he see, or even hope for, a living leader able to meet Lehman's definition of the Carlylesque hero, one gifted with the understanding, foresight, and ability to make good his excellent intentions. What the poet saw, instead, was the corruption, depravity, and hypocrisy which, as fifteen years before in the letter to the bishop of Llandaff, he still saw as natural and inevitable concomitants to high position, high authority, or popular acclaim. The basic law of leadership, said Wordsworth in the *Cintra* tract, is this: "Power of mind is wanting, where there is power of place" (*Cintra,* p. 130). Furthermore, he added, "There is an unconquerable tendency in all power ... to injure the mind of him who exercises that power; so much so, that best natures cannot escape the evil of such alliance" (*Cintra,* p. 139). The true spirit of love does not remain with people who gain power. Wordsworth saw this spirit as common "in a Man, a Citizen, or a Sage," but extinct in "the Political or Military Functionary" (*Cintra,* p. 139). Much of the blame for this condition seemed to the poet to lie with the common and indiscriminate tendency to a sort of hero worship against which he was on guard—despite the contrary charges of modern critics. He wrote: "The power ... of office, whether the duties be discharged well or

116

ill, will insure a never-failing supply of flattery and praise; and of these—a man (becoming at once double-dealer and dupe) may, without impeachment of his modesty, receive as much as his weakness inclines him to; under the shew that the homage is not offered up to himself, but to that portion of the public dignity which is lodged in his person" (*Cintra*, p. 139).

The kind of insight, foresight, and understanding which Carlyle ascribed to great men Wordsworth found incompatible with positions of leadership. These qualities were only to be found "in the walks of common life" (*Cintra*, p. 137). They grew out of a knowledge of human nature which depended for its existence on close association with common humanity. Clearly the theories of Carlyle and Wordsworth are contrary. Those very qualities and virtues which the former saw as characteristic of great men who rise above the rest of mankind the latter saw as diminishing in proportion to the level of distinction attained. Specifically, said the author of the *Cintra* tract, in a long passage which bears quotation in full, positions of *political* power diminish those "heroic" qualities:

It is plain à *priori* that the minds of Statesmen and Courtiers are unfavourable to the growth of this knowledge [of human nature]. For they are in a situation exclusive and artificial; which has the further disadvantage, that it does not separate men from men by collateral partitions which leave, along with difference, a sense of equality—that they, who are divided, are yet upon the same level; but by a degree of superiority which can scarcely fail to be accom-

117

panied with more or less of pride. This situation therefore must be eminently unfavourable for the reception and establishment of that knowledge which is founded not upon things but upon sensations; sensations which are general, and under general influences (and this it is which makes them what they are, and gives them their importance);—not upon things which may be *brought;* but upon sensations which must be *met.* Passing by the kindred and usually accompanying influence of birth in a certain rank—and, where education has been pre-defined from childhood for the express purpose of future political power, the tendency of such education to warp (and therefore weaken) the intellect;—we may join at once, with the privation which I have been noticing, a delusion equally common. It is this: that practical Statesmen assume too much credit to themselves for their ability to see into the motives and manage the selfish passions of their immediate agents and dependants; and for the skill with which they baffle or resist the aims of their opponents. A promptness in looking through the most superficial part of the characters of those men—who, by the very circumstances of their contending ambitiously for the rewards and honours of government, are separated from the mass of the society to which they belong—is mistaken for a knowledge of human kind. Hence, where higher knowledge is a prime requisite, they not only are unfurnished; but, being unconscious that they are so, they look down contemptuously upon those who endeavour to supply (in some degree) their want. —The instincts of natural and

118

social man; the deeper emotions; the simpler feelings; the spacious range of the disinterested imagination; the pride in country for country's sake, when to serve has not been a formal profession—and the mind is therefore left in a state of dignity only to be surpassed by having served nobly and generously; the instantaneous accomplishment in which they start up who, upon a searching call, stir for the land which they love—not from personal motives, but for a reward which is undefined and cannot be missed; the solemn fraternity which a great nation composes—gathered together, in a stormy season, under the shade of ancestral feeling; the delicacy of moral honour which pervades the minds of a people, when despair has been suddenly thrown off and expectations are lofty; the apprehensiveness to a touch unkindly or irreverent, where sympathy is at once exacted as a tribute and welcomed as a gift; the power of injustice and inordinate calamity to transmute, to invigorate, and to govern—to sweep away the barriers of opinion—to reduce under submission passions purely evil—to exalt the nature of indifferent qualities, and to render them fit companions for the absolute virtues with which they are summoned to associate—to consecrate passions which, if not bad in themselves, are of such temper that, in the calm of ordinary life, they are rightly deemed so—to correct and embody these passions—and, without weakening them (nay, with tenfold addition to their strength), to make them worthy of taking their place as the advanced guard of hope, when a sublime movement of deliverance is to be

119

originated;—these arrangements and resources of nature, these ways and means of society, have so little connection with those others upon which a ruling minister of a long-established government is accustomed to depend; these—elements as it were of a universe, functions of a living body—are so opposite, in their mode of action, to the formal machine which it has been his pride to manage;—that he has but a faint perception of their immediate efficacy; knows not the facility with which they assimilate with other powers; nor the property by which such of them—as, from necessity of nature, must change or pass away—will, under wise and fearless management, surely generate lawful successors to fill their place when their appropriate work is performed. (*Cintra,* pp. 134-36)

Men in positions of leadership lose contact not only with that common human virtue and strength which is essential to Carlyle's great man but even with nature herself, perhaps a still greater loss according to Wordsworth's thinking. In describing this other important loss, the poet seems to have had the leaders of the French Revolution especially in mind:

Of the majority of men, who are usually found in high stations under old governments, it may without injustice be said; that, when they look about them in times (alas! too rare) which present the glorious product of such agency to their eyes, they have not a right to say—with a dejected man in the midst of the

120

woods, the rivers, the mountains, the sunshine, and shadows of some transcendant landscape—

"I see, not feel, how beautiful they are:"

These spectators neither see nor feel. And it is from the blindness and insensibility of these, and the train whom they draw along with them, that the throes of nations have been so ill recompensed by the births which have followed; and that revolutions, after passing from crime to crime and from sorrow to sorrow, have often ended in throwing back such heavy reproaches of delusiveness upon their first promises. (*Cintra,* pp. 136-37)

Wordsworth may even have achieved what seems a touch of ironic humor when, after the foregoing analyses of the failures of leadership, he added: "I am satisfied that no enlightened Patriot will impute to me a wish to disparage the characters of men high in authority, or to detract from the estimation which is fairly due to them. My purpose is to guard against unreasonable expectations" (*Cintra,* p. 137).

Having established the causes for the failure of leadership, Wordsworth described in many places in the tract the corruption he saw in high places. The inevitable accouterments of "the heads of the British army and nation" were not the characteristices of heroes. Wordsworth saw them instead with "their forms, their impediments, their rotten customs and precedents, their narrow desires, their busy and purblind fears" (*Cintra,* p. 127). The corruption and cynicism of the ministry of England were apparent to him at the time of the firing of the celebration cannons in London just prior to the release of the terms of the Convention of Cintra (*Cintra,* p. 99), and in the official inquiry into the generals' conduct (*Cintra,* p. 100). The poet was no hero-worshipper. He called on his countrymen not to grant such men the "deference" they claimed due them—"founded upon reputation, even when it is spurious (as much of the reputation of men high in power must necessarily be; their errors being veiled and palliated by the authority attached to their office)" (*Cintra,* p. 132).

It was not because they were English that the leaders of the poet's country were thus corrupt but because they occupied high places. Wordsworth did not fully accept the distinction claimed by General Moore for Iberian leaders but insisted that leaders in any land, even such favored and inspired nations as Spain and Portugal at the time of the uprisings there, could be affected by the same inherent "weakness" of the highly placed (*Cintra,* p. 39). The wisdom and strength which comes from the heart gave "the People of Madrid, and Corunna, and Ferrol" courage to gain victory or to bear defeat; when there was "failure" it was "with those who stood higher in the scale" (*Cintra,* p. 170).

Particularly does the *Cintra* tract make clear that Wordsworth held no hope of finding one of Carlyle's great men in the military forces. The lessons of the recent past, of the convention, of the court of inquiry, all pointed to one conclusion: "The British Army swarms with those who are incompetent" (*Cintra,* p. 151). As with other men in high places, it was the training which inevitably accompanies their positions, the poet believed, which makes incapable of true greatness a nation's military leaders. Referring to the testimony given in the court of inquiry, he wrote:

> Let any one read the evidence ... and he will there see, how much the intellectual and moral constitution of many of our military officers, has suffered by a profession, which, if not counteracted by admonitions willingly listened to, and by habits of meditation, does, more than any other, denaturalize—and therefore degrade the human being;—he will note with sorrow, how faint are their sympathies with the best feelings, and how dim their apprehension of some of the most awful truths, relating to the happiness and dignity of man in society. (*Cintra*, p. 69)

Instead of genuine qualities of leadership, military leaders possess immense arrogance which leads them naturally to trample, as in the Convention of Cintra, "upon the most sacred rights" (*Cintra*, p. 86). It is in their interest, so they believe, to undermine the faith of men in any power other than military. They always deny the "moral superiority inherent in the cause of Freedom" because it seems to make them less important. Wordsworth saw clearly this selfish attempt to conceal powerful truths:

> This paramount efficacy of moral causes is not willingly admitted by persons high in the profession of arms; because it seems to diminish their value in society—by taking from the importance of their art: but the truth is indisputable: and those Generals are

123

as blind to their own interests as to the interests of their country, who, by submitting to inglorious treaties or by other misconduct, hazard the breaking down of those personal virtues in the men under their command—to which they themselves, as leaders, are mainly indebted for the fame which they acquire. (*Cintra*, p. 181)

In the poet's mind, then, it was inevitable that high military position, like all elevation above general humanity, produced corruption and arrogance and selfishness. But of one would-be hero, Wordsworth had something more to say. Sir Arthur Wellesley, subject to the same failings from which any man in his position must suffer, showed by his conduct in Portugal that he also had personal failings of a serious nature. Wellesley's gratuitous insults to his allies and compliments to his foes proved his insensitivity, a quality, said the poet, which "affords too strong suspicion of a deadness to the moral interests of the cause . . . and of such a want of sympathy with the just feelings of his injured Ally as could exist only in a mind narrowed by exclusive and overweening attention to the *military* character, led astray by vanity, or hardened by general habits of contemptuousness" (*Cintra*, p. 48). This particular English commander embodied all that was wrong with all commanders, but he added to those wrongs personal traits of his own which made him, in fact, an enemy to the best interests of his own nation. Wordsworth wrote of these things before Wellesley was returned to the Peninsula to replace General Moore, who was killed in January, 1809. But rumors of the return

124

were already in the air, and the poet expressed his "fear of future consequences" from the command of such a man:

> Here was a man, who, having not any fellow-feeling with the people whom he had been commissioned to aid, could not know where their strength lay, and therefore could not turn it to account, nor by his example call it forth or cherish it; . . . if his future conduct should be in the same spirit, he must be a blighting wind wherever his influence was carried: for he had neither felt the wrongs of his allies nor been induced by common worldly prudence to affect to feel them, or at least to disguise his insensibility; and therefore what could follow, but, in despite of victory and outward demonstrations of joy, inward disgust and depression? (*Cintra,* p. 49)

Although Wordsworth, thus, saw no possibility of the arising of a living hero to guide even the best cause in his day, he saw three bases of hope for such a cause stemming from his view of the nature of leaders and leadership. The first such basis is that, while he believed in no living heroes, the poet believed in dead ones. Death can convert a man of strong principles into the kind of leader whose guidance for his people can be incorruptible. This faith was that upon which two sonnets composed in 1802 had been based, the famous apostrophe to Milton and the lines beginning "Great men have been among us." [12] Similarly, the "ancient Heroes" of book 10 of the 1805 *Prelude* spoke with a "great voice" but one that issued

[12] Ibid., pp. 116-17.

exclusively "from out the tombs"; and the "great Society
... / The noble Living and the noble Dead" would be composed of dead heroes and living followers.[13] In the *Cintra*
tract he wrote of the "solace, which is vouchsafed only
to such nations as can recal to memory the illustrious
deeds of their ancestors" (*Cintra,* p. 37). The people of
the Peninsula, he said, had found such solace and by it
had been inspired to rise up against the French tyranny:

> The names of Pelayo and The Cid are the watch-
> words of the address to the people of Leon; and they
> are told that to these two deliverers of their country,
> and to the sentiments of enthusiasm which they ex-
> cited in every breast, Spain owes the glory and happi-
> ness which she has *so long* enjoyed. The Biscayans
> are called to cast their eyes upon the ages which are
> past, and they will see their ancestors at one time
> repulsing the Carthaginians, at another destroying the
> hordes of Rome; at one period was granted to them
> the distinction of serving in the van of the army; at
> another the privilege of citizens. (*Cintra,* p. 37)

One recent man whom Wordsworth named as a candidate
to become this kind of guiding spirit from beyond the
grave was the Spaniard José de Palafox who had shown
his greatness in the defense of Saragossa.[14] The poet

[13] *Prelude,* p. 422 (bk. 10, lines 954-55, 968-70)—see note 10, p. 115. Specifically mentioned among the "noble Dead" are Timoleon (p. 422, line 951),
Empedocles, Archimedes, and Theocritus (p. 426, lines 1013, 1014, 1016).

[14] At the time of the composition of *Cintra,* Palafox's fate was unknown and
he was presumed killed at Saragossa. Actually he had been captured by the
French and was held incommunicado for five years; he died in 1847. See the
Hutchinson note, *Poetical Works,* 3:459.

wrote in the tract: "Palafox has taken his place as parent and ancestor of innumerable heroes" (*Cintra,* p. 192). That for Wordsworth the only true hero was a dead hero is apparent from the poet's linking of "martyrdom, and fortitude, and right" in the sonnet which he composed on Palafox at about this same time:

> Ah! where is Palafox? Nor tongue nor pen
> Reports of him, his dwelling or his grave!
> Does yet the unheard-of vessel ride the wave?
> Or is she swallowed up, remote from ken
> Of pitying human-nature? Once again
> Methinks that we shall hail thee, Champion brave,
> Redeemed to baffle that imperial Slave,
> And through all Europe cheer desponding men
> With new-born hope. Unbounded is the might
> Of martyrdom, and fortitude, and right.
> Hark, how thy Country triumphs!—Smilingly
> The Eternal looks upon her sword that gleams,
> Like his own lightning, over mountains high,
> On rampart, and the banks of all her streams.[15]

Another basis for hope which Wordsworth derived from his ideas on leaders and leadership was that those same forces which he saw at work preventing the emergence of great and good men were at work undermining the efforts and power of evil leaders also. Such forces would, he believed, finally cause the destruction of Napoleon. "Every one knows that Despotism, in a general sense, is but another word for weakness" (*Cintra,* p. 146). But Words-

[15] Ibid., p. 135.

worth admitted that Napoleon's regime had immense, though temporary, strength. It was not a regime which grew out of a traditional and enfeebled monarchy, but one "immediately preceded by a popular Constitution" (*Cintra,* p. 146). The officials of the regime were generally able in their offices. And "from the conjunction of absolute civil and military authority in a single Person, there naturally follows promptness of decision; concentration of effort; rapidity of motion; and confidence that the movements made will be regularly supported." And from such causes Napoleon derived "for the purposes of external annoyance, a preternatural vigour" (*Cintra,* pp. 146-147). Moreover, Napoleon's personal character was another source of temporary strength: "For . . . the personal character of the Chief: I shall at present content myself with noting (to prevent misconception) that this basis is not laid in any superiority of talents in him, but in his utter rejection of the restraints of morality—in wickedness which acknowledges no limit but the extent of its own power. Let any one reflect a moment: and he will feel that a new world of forces is opened to a Being who has made this desperate leap. It is a tremendous principle to be adopted, and steadily adhered to, by a man in the station which Buonaparte occupies; and he has taken the full benefit of it" (*Cintra,* p. 147). But the poet also saw, and endeavored to teach his countrymen, that this real but temporary vigor was actually "weak, perilous, and self-destructive" (*Cintra,* p. 147). Napoleon's eager greed had led him to despise the people from whom lasting strength could come. In his conquest of the Peninsula, the French emperor had trampled on the people of Spain and Portugal, had rejected their claims to independent nationhood, had instead chosen as his allies the degenerate former rulers of those people. Wordsworth saw it as Napoleon's first great mistake—a fatal one, he predicted:

> The government which had been exercised under the name of the old Monarchy of Spain—this government, imbecile even to dotage, whose very selfishness was destitute of vigour, had been removed; taken laboriously and foolishly by the plotting Corsican to his own bosom; in order that the world might see, more triumphantly set forth than since the beginning of things had ever been seen before, to what degree a man of bad principles is despicable—though of great power—working blindly against his own purposes. It was a high satisfaction to behold demonstrated ... to what a narrow domain of knowledge the intellect of a Tyrant must be confined; that, if the gate by which wisdom enters has never been opened, that of policy will surely find moments when it will shut itself ... imperiously and obstinately. To the eyes of the very peasant in the field, this sublime truth was laid open— not only that a Tyrant's domain of knowledge is narrow, but melancholy as narrow; inasmuch as—from all that is lovely, dignified, or exhilarating in the prospect of human nature—he is inexorably cut off; and therefore he is inwardly helpless and forlorn. (*Cintra,* pp. 123-24)

Napoleon's flaws were those of every leader coupled with the eventual debility of every evil cause. The poet found reason for great hope in "the weakness of him who ...

thus counteracted himself" (*Cintra*, p. 124).

According to Wordsworth, true strength lies with the people; and leaders who rely on this popular strength can gain wisdom unattainable to ordinary leaders. Here was the surest basis of hope of all. Real heroism belongs to the common people only, but men who aspire to greatness can offset some of the bad effects of high position by a communing contact with this democratic source of power and knowledge. Writing of "those who are in authority," the poet said: "There is . . . an inherent impossibility that they should be equal to the arduous duties which have devolved upon them: but it is not unreasonable to hope that something higher might be aimed at; and that the People might see, upon great occasions,—in the practice of its Rulers—a more adequate reflection of its own wisdom and virtue" (*Cintra,* pp. 142-43). What is true of political leaders is equally true of military commanders, as the Convention of Cintra and succeeding events proved to the poet: "These are times also in which, if we may judge from the proceedings and result of the Court of Inquiry, the heads of the army, more than at any other period, stand in need of being taught wisdom by the voice of the people" (*Cintra,* p. 68). The very elevation of high position which cuts leaders off from communion with human nature makes imperative their listening to the wisdom of the people. "There are promptings of wisdom," Wordsworth claimed, "from the penetralia of human nature, which a people can hear, though the wisest of their practical Statesmen be deaf towards them" (*Cintra,* p. 9). Particularly in times of crisis must. leaders be attuned to these promptings from the people. The peninsular in-

surrections exemplified such occasions. The people of
Great Britain at that time knew more about values and
principles than their leaders. Had the popular judgment
been heeded there could have been no Convention of
Cintra:

> Every human being in these islands was unsettled;
> the most slavish broke loose as from fetters; and
> there was not an individual—it need not be said of
> heroic virtue, but of ingenuous life and sound discre-
> tion—who, if his father, his son, or his brother, or if
> the flower of his house had been in that army, would
> not rather that they had perished, and the whole body
> of their countrymen, their companions in arms, had
> perished to a man, than that a treaty should have
> been submitted to upon such conditions. This was the
> feeling of the people; an awful feeling: and it is from
> these oracles that rulers are to learn wisdom. (*Cin-
> tra,* p. 110)

The English leaders, however, were not attuned to the
people. For his own country, Wordsworth saw this principle as still only a hope, not yet a fact. But proof that the
principle was valid was afforded him by the success of the
peninsular uprisings. The actions of the revolutionary
governments there proved that many peninsular leaders
recognized and relied on the strength of the people. Those
leaders demonstrated the "sympathies which prove that a
government is paternal,—that it makes one family with the
people" (*Cintra,* p. 82). The demonstration, while it gave
hope to Wordsworth and to all Englishmen, brought suc-

131

cess—the realization of the people's wishes for independence—to the Peninsula: "These events ... have shewn
that the cause of the People ... is safe while it remains
not only in the bosom but in the hands of the People; or
(what amounts to the same thing) in those of a government
which, being truly *from* the People, is faithfully *for*
them" (*Cintra,* pp. 155-56).

Wordsworth's faith, as he expressed it in the *Cintra*
tract, lay not in heroes but in the people. He admitted
the strength which great men could acquire, but he saw,
too, their inherent weaknesses that made such strength
unreliable and transitory. His thinking on this subject
was reinforced by the events surrounding the Convention
of Cintra, and the lessons which he then learned were
never forgotten by him. In 1827, shortly following the
publication of the second volume of Robert Southey's
History of the Peninsular War, in which the reigning
poet laureate showed that he had become a hero-worshipper, Wordsworth wrote him:

> Edith thanked you, in my name, for your valuable
> present of the "Peninsular War." I have read it with
> great delight: it is beautifully written, and a most
> interesting story. I did not notice a single sentiment
> or opinion that I could have wished away but one—
> where you support the notion that, if the Duke of
> Wellington had not lived and commanded, Buonaparte
> must have continued the master of Europe. I do not
> object to this from any dislike I have to the Duke, but
> from a conviction—I trust, a philosophic one—that
> Providence would not allow the upsetting of so dia-

bolical a system as Buonaparte's to depend upon the existence of any individual. Justly was it observed by Lord Wellesley, that Buonaparte was of an order of minds that created for themselves great reverses. He might have gone further, and said that it is of the nature of tyranny to work to its own destruction.[16]

[16] *Letters: Later Years.* 1:264.

6

The Results of the *Cintra* Tract

"We have heard from several quarters that the pamphlet has made considerable impression—I mean among a few."[1] Thus did Dorothy Wordsworth, writing to De Quincey, describe the effect of the *Cintra* tract a month after its appearance. One of those who were impressed was Coleridge, who said, "I have not often met with a book at once so profound & so eloquent."[2] But Coleridge shared with Dorothy a sense of being "among a few" in his admiration. To Daniel Stuart, who confidently looked forward to a second printing of the tract, he wrote on June 13, 1809: "I have just read Wordsworth's pamphlet— & more than fear that your friendly Expectations of it's Sale & Influence have been too sanguine. Had I not known the Author, I would willingly have travelled from St Michael's Mount to Johnny Groat's House on a pilgrimage to see & reverence him— but from the Public I am apprehensive."[3]

Catherine Clarkson was another ardent admirer of the tract, but she too feared that there would not be many

---

[1] *Letters: Middle Years,* 1:331.
[2] Griggs, *Letters of Coleridge,* 3:217.
[3] Ibid., pp. 213-14.

other admirers. To Henry Crabb Robinson she wrote:
"There are passages that roused me like a sudden blast
from a trumpet. 'How long' exclaimed my soul 'have I
been sleeping in the dust' & and immediately took wing &
soared aloft." Then she added: "Yet it is melancholy to
think how few will read that book with other than feelings
of contempt."[4] She took the trouble to send a copy of the
tract to Thomas Robinson and wrote him her own opinion
of it: "It was given into my hands with these words 'It is
not english there is no english feeling in it.' I fear this is
true but it would have been english 150 years ago & I
trust that it will yet be english. At least I desire to be
cut off from all hopes of posterity rather than that any
descendant of mine should not reverence the sentiments
contained in that book or want courage to act up to them."[5]
And in his turn Thomas Robinson praised the tract too.
Of Wordsworth he wrote, "In prose he is to me beautifully
perspiccous [sic]." But he added, a little defensively:
"Indeed there are few readers, I take for granted, whose
judgment is worth anything, but will admit his superiority
in this respect—the impression left upon my mind after
perusing his 'Convention of Cintra' will remain as long as
I retain any thing."[6]

Sir Walter Scott, after reading the two sections of the
tract which appeared in the newspaper, wrote Southey:
"I have read Wordsworth's lucubrations in the Courier,
and much agree with him. Alas, we want everything but

---

[4] Morley, *Correspondence of Robinson*, 1:55.

[5] Ibid., pp. 54-55. This passage is badly garbled, by attributing the words
and the sentiment "It is not English" to Catherine Clarkson herself, in F. M.
Todd, *Politics and the Poet: A Study of Wordsworth* (London: Methuen &
Co., 1957), p. 141.

[6] Morley, *Correspondence of Robinson*, 2:539.

courage and virtue in this desperate contest.... We
can only fight like mastiffs, boldly, blindly, and faithfully."[7] And Charles Lamb wrote to Coleridge early in
June: "I was very glad to see Wordsworth's book adver-
tised; I am to have it to-morrow lent me, and if Wordsworth don't send me an order for one upon Longman, I
will buy it. It is greatly extolled and liked by all who have
seen it."[8] Still the general feeling about the *Cintra*
tract seems to have been that it was excellent but not
likely to have much influence. Anthony Robinson wrote
Henry Crabb Robinson (no relation)[9] of his response to
the work in terms which Wordsworth later said pleased
him because he felt the writer had understood him very
well.[10] Of the author of the tract Anthony Robinson wrote:
"In true poetical inspiration & the bursting language of
passion, he is infinitely above Burke." He added, however:
"The man of passion, (one of ten thousand) of high moral
enthusiasm, is the only man who will relish his work, &
indeed to him, it will be the Bible of his Life. He will
have but few admirers, but those will salute him with
ardent & eternal admiration."[11]

[7] Lockhart, *Life of Scott,* 2:117.

[8] E. V. Lucas, ed., *The Works of Charles and Mary Lamb,* 7 vols. (New York: G. P. Putnam's Sons, 1905), 6:400. Lamb did read *Cintra,* but he had to buy his own copy. Wordsworth wrote Wrangham before the tract was published that he would not order any copies for friends. (See *Letters: Middle Years,* 1:290.) Lamb's favorable reaction upon reading was also tinged with the same sentiment of being one of few. Lamb wrote Coleridge, on October 30, 1809, of the tract: "Its power over me was like that which Milton's pamphlets must have had on his contemporaries, who were tuned to them." See Lucas, *Works of Lamb,* 6:404.

[9] Moorman, *Wordsworth: Later Years,* p. 154, errs in thinking them brothers.

[10] Edith J. Morley, ed., *Blake, Coleridge, Wordsworth, Lamb, Etc., Being Selections from the Remains of Henry Crabb Robinson* (New York: Longmans, Green & Co., 1922), p. 56.

[11] Morley, *Correspondence of Robinson,* 1:55.

Indeed the ardent admiration was not universal. Thomas Quayle, who also wrote his opinion of the tract to Henry Crabb Robinson, felt that Wordsworth overestimated the moral motives of the Peninsular insurgents "in these degenerate Days." But his main quarrel was with the poet's style. "The matter is excellently good of this Pamphlet," he wrote. "But as to the dress in w[ch] these Thoughts are clothed, I think it I confess, most slovenly— Nay I dont know that I ever read a *worse* writer than Mr. W." He disliked the long sentences of the tract, and he complained of the poet's use of such words as *wherein* and the plural *ones*. Quayle concluded: "I don't know who may be the Author's Model:—His Style resembles the worst of Burke's,—But I do not expect that he himself will be a Model to any body else." Robinson noted that Quayle was already prejudiced against Wordsworth's poetry and that the letter in which the foregoing comments were contained was preserved "as a specimen of the times."[12] But similar criticism came from many sources. The anonymous review in the *British Critic* of September, 1809, was largely favorable to Wordsworth: "Upon the whole, the generous spirit which this pamphlet breathes, and the knowledge of human nature, which in many passages, it evinces, claim attention and applause." Yet the reviewer felt it necessary to add that "the Author's enthusiasm is not, we think, void of extravagance" and "his style, though it often interests by eloquence, as frequently fatigues by prolixity."[13] Henry Crabb Robin-

[12] Ibid., pp. 59, 60.
[13] Cited in Elsie Smith, *An Estimate of William Wordsworth by His Contemporaries, 1793-1822* (Oxford: Basil Blackwell & Mott, 1932), p. 118. Smith's

son himself expressed, for all his admiration of the tract, mild disapproval of its style. In his review of *Cintra* in the *London Review* of November, 1809, the first article to be published over his name, Robinson wrote:

> Wordsworth will not possess, or merit to possess, the popularity of Burke, who, being schooled in the House of Commons, always laboured to make himself intelligible to the lowest capacity. Wordsworth writes from the woods and lakes, and seems content to be understood and relished by a few like himself; his thoughts are great, but sometimes obscure; his genius is original, and therefore unaccommodating; his style is involved and uncouth, when not impassioned; and he resembles a man who limps till he has walked himself warm: hence the latter half of the pamphlet is better than the former, and he repeats, at the close, the thoughts of the beginning, with great improvement.[14]

Others of Wordsworth's friends expressed similar reservations. Even as he was recommending the tract to his acquaintances, Coleridge wrote that in his opinion "the effect of national enthusiasm in the Spanish People is

---

work is especially valuable for its providing easy access to this and other reviews otherwise not readily available.

[14] Ibid., pp. 121-22. Robinson later wrote of the results of both this review and the tract: "My review gained me, I believe, very little credit—not with Wordsworth, though eulogistic. Nor did his pamphlet obtain with the larger public all the honour which it merited." See Edith J. Morley, ed., *Henry Crabb Robinson on Books and Their Writers*, 3 vols. (London: J. M. Dent & Sons, 1938), 1:13.

somewhat too much *idealized.*" And if not for his own
taste at least for ordinary readers, Coleridge thought the
style of the tract too ornate with its "alarmingly long"
sentences and what he considered De Quincey's confusing
punctuation.[15] With these latter objections Southey
agreed, predicting that such defects in the tract would
hamper its effectiveness. To Scott he wrote:

> Wordsworth's pamphlet will fail of producing any
> general effect, because the sentences are long and
> involved; and his friend, De Quincey, who corrected
> the press, has rendered them more obscure by an
> unusual system of punctuation. This fault will out-
> weigh all its merits. The public never can like any
> thing which they feel it difficult to understand....
> I impute Wordsworth's want of perspicuity to two
> causes,—his admiration of Milton's prose, and his
> habit of dictating instead of writing: if he were his
> own scribe his eye would tell him where to stop; but,
> in dictating, his own thoughts are to himself familiarly
> intelligible, and he goes on, unconscious either of the
> length of the sentence, or the difficulty a common
> reader must necessarily find in following its meaning
> to the end, and unravelling all its involutions.[16]

[15] Griggs, *Letters of Coleridge,* 3:216, 214.

[16] *Life and Correspondence of Southey,* 3:246-47. Besides the reasons given
by Coleridge, Southey, and others for what might be called the popular
failure of *Cintra,* recent critics have suggested other causes. R. J. White in his
introduction to *Political Tracts of Wordsworth, Coleridge and Shelley* (Cambridge: Cambridge University Press, 1953), p. xxxii, sees a "failure in comprehension" and "a failure in philosophy," attributable to "the triumph of feeling over intellectual grasp." And Herbert Lindenberger, *On Wordsworth's
"Prelude"* (Princeton: Princeton University Press, 1963), p. 266, writes that
the poet's conception of politics was entirely "in terms of abstract principles"
and that the tract does not explore "the gap between principles and actuali-
ties."

Wordsworth's own hopes for results from the *Cintra* tract seem not to have been very different from the pessimistic expectations of these friends. The long delay in the publication of the work, he knew, had relegated the Convention of Cintra to that special oblivion to which public opinion assigns any scandal which is followed by still more entertaining scandals. The affairs of the duke of York and the adventuress Mary Ann Clarke, which led to a public inquiry and the duke's resignation in March, 1809, as commander in chief of the army, had captured whatever public attention might have remained for the events in the Peninsula of the previous summer.[17] Wordsworth thus wrote to Francis Wrangham a month before the tract even appeared, speaking not as an author who shortly expected to make a stir but rather relieved at having "discharged this debt to my Country, and to the virtuous of all Countries." It was, wrote the poet, "done according to the best light of my Conscience." His expectations were a mingling of hope and fear: "It is indeed very imperfect, and will, I fear be little read; but, if it is read, it cannot I hope fail of doing some good."[18]

At any rate, a principle which appears repeatedly in the tract itself, as shown in the preceding chapter, is that it is not public opinion which needs to be reformed but the opinions and actions of public officials. With the effect of the *Cintra* tract on the leaders of nations rather than on public opinion Wordsworth was concerned, if not hopeful. He ordered copies of the tract sent to the ambassadors of Spain and Portugal, "and to three or four other public

[17] See Dicey, Introduction, *Cintra*, pp. xviii-xix.
[18] *Letters: Middle Years,* 1:290.

men, and Members of Parliament."[19] But even here the poet's chief interest seems to have been not in changing the course of government policy but in setting the record straight. In asking De Quincey to have copies of the tract delivered to the peninsular representatives, Wordsworth instructed him: "In your note to Spanish and Portuguese Ambassadors, pray state that one of my principal objects was to refute the calumnies which selfish men had circulated in this country against those two nations."[20] For this purpose, the poet even briefly considered with De Quincey having portions of the tract translated into Spanish—"such . . . as were likely to be of any use." And it appears that he was thinking again of clearing reputations when he told De Quincey: "As to the pamphlet, you will send it to whomsoever you think proper. As I have defended the City, perhaps a few copies might with advantage be sent to the leading Members there."[21]

Even in aiming at this limited target, Wordsworth seems not to have hit his mark. In a letter to Dorothy Wordsworth sent near the end of May, 1809, De Quincey promised that copies of the tract, bound in special covers, would be delivered "to the Spanish and Portuguese Ambassadors" and to other Spanish officials.[22] There is probably no reason to doubt that this promise was fulfilled, but no record of the tract's being received by the embassies of Spain and Portugal exists.[23] Whatever results the poet

[19] Ibid.
[20] Ibid., p. 273.
[21] Ibid., p. 266.
[22] Jordan, *De Quincey to Wordsworth,* p. 181.
[23] Magalhães Feu, secretary to the embassy of Portugal in London, informed this writer in a letter dated July 6, 1967, that no record of the tract exists in that embassy. Similarly, Eduardo Toda, cultural counselor at the embassy of Spain in London, informed me, in his letter of July 14, 1967, that

hoped to achieve through the embassies apparently never materialized.[24] Evidence that he had no real expectation of influencing the conduct of government policy appears in his cool response to Lady Beaumont's news that Foreign Minister George Canning agreed that the tract was written "with the bone of truth." For government ministers Wordsworth showed that he had little hope and considerable contempt. He wrote back to Lady Beaumont: "The misfortune is, with persons in Mr. Canning's situation, it is impossible to know when they speak with *sincerity*."[25]

It may be said, then, in summary of the response which greeted the *Cintra* tract when it first appeared that it was chiefly those who already knew and admired Wordsworth who admired his tract; and even some of them had reservations. But neither the poet nor his friends seemed disappointed or surprised by such a response. Dorothy Wordsworth was not expressing the frustration of great expectations come to nothing when she wrote nearly three months after the appearance of the tract: "All the judicious seem to admire it. Many are astonished with the wisdom of it—but nobody buys!! An edition of 500 is not yet sold."[26] Indeed that first edition was never ex-

---

his embassy has no record of any kind concerning the tract. Further, at his kind request, the Ministry of Foreign Affairs in Madrid checked and found, as reported to me in a letter of August 22, 1967, that the tract does not appear in the records of the ministry.

[24] It is interesting to note, however, that the Spanish critic Salvador de Madariaga, who believes that it is Wordsworth's devotion to virtue above art that has made the poet so little read and appreciated in Spain, says that this very devotion to virtue is "on a noble and elevated plane when it inspires his courageous Tract against the Convention of Cintra." See "The Case of Wordsworth," in *Shelley and Calderon and Other Essays on English and Spanish Poetry* (London: Constable & Co., 1920), p. 183.

[25] *Letters: Middle Years*, 1:372.

[26] Ibid., p. 340.

hausted. One year after it was published, the tract had
sold only 238 copies. Considering the fact that the public
furor over the Convention of Cintra was long dead, however, the poet would probably have agreed with a modern
scholar who writes: "The sales were remarkably good.
Here, as in the cases of his other earlier publications,
Wordsworth was reaching a genuinely interested and
appreciative body of purchasers."[27]

Early in this century the historian Mario Méndez
Bejarano described a curious old drawing which he had
seen displayed in the Doblado Bookstore in Madrid. It
depicted Napoleon carrying a pen marked "deceit" and
ascending with his admirers a stairway on the steps of
which lay blindfolded persons, each of whom represented
a different European nation. Arriving at the step of Spain,
the emperor stopped when a woman representing Seville
appeared and challenged him. Napoleon's brother and
several of his battlefield commanders here fell in fright
from the stairway. Next appeared an Englishman, bearing
a banner marked "reputation"; this man removed the
blindfolds from the eyes of the nations, allowing them to
see clearly what had happened in Spain. Napoleon, in
fury, fell and dragged with him his allies and his deceit-
ful pen.[28]

Whoever the Englishman who marched alone but vic-
toriously under the banner of reputation in the drawing
may have been, he was not William Wordsworth. There is
no evidence that Wordsworth's attempt to open the eyes

[27] John Edwin Wells, "Printer's Bills for Coleridge's *Friend* and Wordsworth's *Cintra*," *Studies in Philology* 36 (1939): 522.
[28] Mario Méndez Bejarano, *Historia de los afrancesados* (Madrid: Impresa
de Felipe Peña Cruz, 1912), p. 284.

of Europe in the *Cintra* tract had any success. To make any claim at all for identifiable results from the tract seems dangerous. Nevertheless, there is in a few scholars a tendency to let their enthusiasm for *Cintra* lead them into the danger. Dicey acknowledges that the tract, "impressive as it is, could never have been easy reading; its sale was small; it certainly was not read by the mass of English electors." Yet he feels that the *Cintra* tract "did produce one immediate effect of untold value," even if it failed to make the kind of change in public opinion which Edmund Burke had made twenty years before with his *Reflections on the Revolution in France.*[29] Wordsworth's work, says Dicey,

> brought into one line every man throughout the United Kingdom who detested the despotism of Bonaparte and recognized the duty of England to save herself by an unappeasable war against the aggression of the French Emperor, and thereby to secure the independence of every European State menaced or enslaved by the gigantic power of the Empire.... Tories, such as Scott, John Wilson, and Castlereagh, joined hands with revolutionists, such as had been Wordsworth and Coleridge, who had deprecated or detested a war which threatened the independence, and even the existence, of France. For English Tories and revolutionists alike could all sympathize with countries which at every risk dared to oppose the attacks of a foreign despot.... The war was transformed from a war against France into

[29] Dicey, *Statesmanship of Wordsworth,* p. 94.

a national war for the defence of England. This transformation was due in no small degree to Wordsworth's
patriotic sonnets and to his *Tract on the Convention
of Cintra.* [30]

Dicey says further that the tract had another notable
result, the second one lasting whereas the first was immediate: "The pamphlet's permanent effect lies in its
containing the doctrine of Nationalism" which was to
guide English foreign policy throughout the nineteenth
century. Comments Dicey, "The policy of our country,
in so far as it coincided with the statesmanship of Wordsworth, was during that century markedly successful; in
so far as it deviated from his statesmanship it ended in
failure, or at best in very dubious success." [31] Kenneth
MacLean agrees in general with Dicey's generous view of
the results of the *Cintra* tract. The poet, he says, made
a great contribution "at the critical time when England
needed 'a cause' on which to fight the Napoleonic empire."
Wordsworth's writings were very influential in helping
"England find the cause of a Europe of free and independent
nations." [32]

The influence or lack of it of a man or a work of literature on the course of history can be very difficult to
ascertain. But there remains apparent too much in the
history of the nineteenth century, too much even in the
conduct of the war against Napoleon after 1809 (e.g., the
return of Wellesley to Spain, the reinstating of the Duke

[30] Ibid., pp. 94-95.
[31] Introduction, *Cintra*, pp. xxxii-xxxiii.
[32] Kenneth MacLean, *Agrarian Age: A Background for Wordsworth* (New
Haven: Yale University Press, 1950), p. 101.

of York as commander in chief in 1811), which would have provoked the expounder of the principles of the *Cintra* tract to dismay rather than to pride of accomplishment. The claims for significant and decisive results from the tract, as Moorman says, are "unsupported by any proof."[33] Perhaps no less important, claims for direct political or military results from the tract seem inconsistent with Wordsworth's own stated intentions, or at least his expectations, for his work. These seem accurately summed up by Christopher Wordsworth, who wrote of his uncle's *Cintra* tract: "The author composed the work in the discharge of what he regarded a sacred duty, and for the permanent benefit of society, rather than with a view to any immediate results."[34]

Probably the best statements of all on what the poet felt as he worked on the tract and what he expected to come from it, as well as a prophetically accurate statement of what the results actually were to be, are found in the two sonnets composed as he was writing the tract, written near the end of 1808. In the first he described his inspiration and the sources from which he drew his thoughts, sources which he believed would make those thoughts triumphant in the long run:

> Not 'mid the World's vain objects that enslave
> The free-born Soul—that World whose vaunted skill
> In selfish interest perverts the will,
> Whose factions lead astray the wise and brave—

[33] Moorman, *Wordsworth: Later Years,* p. 154. Moorman refers specifically to Dicey's claims.

[34] *Memoirs of William Wordsworth,* ed. Christopher Wordsworth, 2 vols. (Boston, 1851), 1:403.

Not there; but in dark wood and rocky cave,
And hollow vale which foaming torrents fill
With omnipresent murmur as they rave
Down their steep beds, that never shall be still:
Here, mighty Nature! in this school sublime
I weigh the hopes and fears of suffering Spain;
For her consult the auguries of time,
And through the human heart explore my way;
And look and listen—gathering, whence I may,
Triumph, and thoughts no bondage can restrain.[35]

The second sonnet was also prompted by thoughts which came to the poet from events in nature, but these thoughts were on the response which Wordsworth believed would greet the *Cintra* tract:

I dropped my pen; and listened to the Wind
That sang of trees up-torn and vessels tost—
A midnight harmony; and wholly lost
To the general sense of men by chains confined
Of business, care, or pleasure; or resigned
To timely sleep. Thought I, the impassioned strain,
Which, without aid of numbers, I sustain,
Like acceptation from the World will find.
Yet some with apprehensive ear shall drink
A dirge devoutly breathed o'er sorrows past;
And to the attendant promise will give heed—
The prophecy,—like that of this wild blast,
Which, while it makes the heart with sadness shrink,
Tells also of bright calms that shall succeed.[36]

[35] *Poetical Works*, 3:128.
[36] Ibid., pp. 128-29.

The response to the tract, Wordsworth foresaw, would be characterized by the indifference of "the general sense of men" but with the attention of "some with apprehensive ear"—without direct and immediate results but with eventual vindication.

7

The *Cintra* Tract: Apostate's Creed?

In discussing with his friend William Mathews the possibility of "setting on foot a monthly Miscellany" in
1794, Wordsworth wanted to be sure that they understood
each other's political sentiments; and he wrote Mathews:
"Here at the very threshold I solemnly affirm that in no
writings of mine will I ever admit of any sentiment which
can have the least tendency to induce my readers to suppose that the doctrines which are now enforced by banish-
ment, imprisonment, &c, &c, are other than pregnant with
every species of misery. You know perhaps already that
I am of that odious class of men called democrats, and of
that class I shall for ever continue."[1] If the poet seems
to have been almost pessimistic—"It was a lamentable
time for man"[2]—he seems nevertheless to have been
sincere. Yet this sentiment as expressed to Mathews,
according to Malcolm Elwin, can only "be read with shame
and sadness in the light of Wordsworth's subsequent
career."[3] Elwin's belief that Wordsworth, known for his

[1] *Early Letters,* pp. 115-16.
[2] *Prelude,* p. 389 (bk. 10, line 384).
[3] Malcolm Elwin, *The First Romantics* (New York: Longmans, Green & Co.,
1948), p. 44.

youthful democratic radicalism, became a conservative in his later years is shared by many Wordsworthian scholars. The testimony of no less a witness than Henry Crabb Robinson is often cited as evidence that the poet's apostasy was admitted even by his defenders in his own day. Robinson wrote Dorothy Wordsworth in 1826: "I assure you it gives me real pain when I think that some future commentator may possibly hereafter write—'This great poet survived to the fifth decennary of the Nineteenth Century, but he appears to have dyed in the year 1814 as far as life consisted in an active sympathy with the temporary welfare of his fellow creatures—He had written heroically & divinely against the tyranny of Napoleon, but was quite indifferent to all the successive tyrannies which disgraced the succeeding times.' "[4] So widespread is the belief in the poet's apostasy from his early principles that a recent study of his politics, far from questioning whether there was such a change, announces as its purpose the attempt to "document Wordsworth's notorious change of political heart."[5] This notorious change in his politics, it has been said, amounted to the final limitation of Wordsworth's social program "to intellectual and

[4] Morley, *Correspondence of Robinson*, 1:153. But it has been shown clearly that Robinson meant that he knew that Wordsworth had stuck to his same principles but feared that others might either misunderstand or intentionally distort the poet's later years. Thus Robinson's remark is often twisted "to support that very accusation of coldness, indifference, and hardening" against which Robinson was defending Wordsworth (Edith C. Batho, *The Later Wordsworth* [Cambridge: Cambridge University Press, 1933], p. 136). C. H. Herford, *Wordsworth* (London: George Routledge & Sons, 1930), p. 193, adds that such misunderstandings as those feared by Robinson could easily arise in men who failed to see or accept Wordsworth's distinction between tyranny imposed from without and that from within (see *Cintra*, pp. 167-68).

[5] Todd, *Politics and the Poet*, p. 11. Todd acknowledges, however (p. 139), the "essential liberal tone of the . . . [*Cintra*] tract."

social mediocrity" resulting from "the timid conventionalism and narrow prejudices of his long old age."[6] The traditional view which accuses the poet of being a lost leader has been not unfairly summed up by Ernest San Juan, Jr., as seeing the author of *Lyrical Ballads, The Prelude,* and the *Cintra* tract become only a "petty propagandist, an orthodox Anglican who repudiated his former individualism to win public acclaim and official recognition from the Establishment."[7]

It is common among believers in Wordsworth's apostasy to attribute the change in his principles to his changing attitudes about France. In book 3 of *The Excursion* (lines 827-30), the Solitary describes these results from the events in France when revolution turned to terror and finally to the tyranny of Napoleon:

—In Britain, ruled a panic dread of change;
The weak were praised, rewarded, and advanced;
And, from the impulse of a just disdain,
Once more did I retire into myself.[8]

These lines, according to Carson C. Hamilton, apply better to the poet himself than to the rest of his countrymen: in reaction to Napoleon, Wordsworth suffered a solidification and became a "confirmed alarmist" in public affairs.[9] Alfred Cobban agrees; the essence of the

---

[6] Laura Johnson Wylie, "The Social Philosophy of Wordsworth," in *Social Studies in English Literature* (Boston: Houghton Mifflin Co., 1916), pp. 132, 165. And Carl R. Woodring, "On Liberty in the Poetry of Wordsworth," *PMLA* 70 (1955): 1047, calls the change in the poet "a curdling within."

[7] Ernest San Juan, Jr., "Wordsworth and Political Commitment," *Dalhousie Review* 45 (1965): 299.

[8] *Poetical Works,* 5:104.

[9] Carson C. Hamilton, *Wordsworth's Decline in Poetic Power: Prophet into High Priest* (New York: Exposition Press, 1963), pp. 15, 17.

apostasy, he says, was the poet's passing "from extreme Francophilism to equally extreme anti-Gallican nationalism."[10] A variation of this theory, as explained by Lehman and Read, is that Wordsworth's remorse over his treatment of Annette Vallon led him to a form of psychological self-defense in which he rejected France and the revolutionary principles which he had learned there and became instead a conservative.[11]

Those believers in the poet's apostasy who see evidence in his work of so thorough and sudden a rejection of his earlier principles agree in finding it particularly in the *Cintra* tract. Chew writes: The "re-orientation of his political and social ideas . . . is marked in the prose tract on *The Convention of Cintra*"—a change which amounted in the poet's life and work after 1809 to anticlimax and decline.[12] Walter Graham describes the apostate Wordsworth as "narrow and hidebound" in politics and "either silent or obstructive" on major public issues, and claims that the *Cintra* tract shows its author to have been moving into religious conformity as well.[13] Lehman agrees that the poet's new doctrine expressing his conservative point of view was delivered in *Cintra*.[14] And Willard L. Sperry calls the ideas in the tract the complete reverse

[10] Alfred Cobban, *Edmund Burke and the Revolt against the Eighteenth Century,* 2d ed. (London: George Allen & Unwin, 1960), p. 144. Brandes, *Naturalism in England,* p. 86, also shares this view.

[11] See Lehman, "Doctrine of Leadership in the Greater Romantic Poets," pp. 639-40, and Read, *Wordsworth,* pp. 233-34. A somewhat more clinical approach is made by A. L. Strout, "Wordsworth's Dessication," *Modern Language Review* 35 (1940): 162-72.

[12] Chew, *Nineteenth Century and After,* p. 1145.

[13] Walter Graham, "The Politics of the Greater Romantic Poets," *PMLA* 36 (1921), 66, 68.

[14] Lehman, "Doctrine of Leadership in the Greater Romantic Poets," pp. 639-40.

of the disdain for the corruption of England expressed by the poet in his letter to Bishop Watson of Llandaff.[15]

By no means do all Wordsworthian scholars agree with the foregoing theories.[16] Before the end of the nineteenth century, William Hale White was defending the poet against the charges of apostasy by an examination of the principles expressed in the poetry.[17] Walter Raleigh, a few years later, claimed that the years of which the *Cintra* tract was the climax did not bring apostasy but philosophical maturity.[18] Another writer early in this century saw Wordsworth's horror at the Convention of Cintra as "not only consistent, but homogeneous" with his views of fifteen years earlier.[19] Edith Batho, in her more recent study which ends in rejecting the charges of apostasy, documents her claim that "much of the criticism of Wordsworth's later years rests on political and religious

[15] Willard L. Sperry, *Wordsworth's Anti-Climax* (Cambridge: Harvard University Press, 1935), p. 67. Sperry sees the apostasy as more a conversion to Burke than a rejection of France. An interesting twist on these theories is provided by George McLean Harper, *William Wordsworth: His Life, Works, and Influence*, 2 vols. (New York: Charles Scribner's Sons, 1923), 2:178, who sees *Cintra* not as a result of apostasy but a cause: the poet's panic at the time of the convention and the exhausting work of writing the tract made him recoil from all recklessness, diminished his interest in reforms, and served "to elevate conservatism into a religion."

[16] Most of these theories were formulated before modern and definitive editions of Wordsworth's letters and poetry were available, a handicap pointed out by Batho, *Later Wordsworth*, p. 181. She, too, wrote before the de Selincourt editions of letters and poems were available, but awareness of the problems (e. g., misdated letters, corrupted texts) seems to have helped her solve them, or at least avoid common pitfalls.

[17] See W. Hale White, *An Examination of the Charge of Apostasy against Wordsworth* (London, 1898).

[18] Walter Raleigh, *Wordsworth* (London: E. Arnold, 1903), p. 53. The maturity was also in the poet's imagination, says Arthur Beatty, *William Wordsworth: His Doctrine and Art in Their Historical Relations* (Madison: University of Wisconsin Press, 1962), pp. 88-89.

[19] David Watson Rannie, *Wordsworth and His Circle* (New York: G. P. Putnam's Sons, 1907), p. 191.

prejudice."[20] From her study of the nature and quantity of the changes made by the poet over the years in *The Prelude,* Mary E. Burton concludes that the evidence supports Batho's view.[21] She wrote of the charges against the poet: "He has been pictured all too often as a stiff-backed old Tory walking idly in the hills near Rydal Mount or sitting at home complacently drinking in the adulation of visitors. In this popular conception, he is supposed to have thought very little for himself, and when he did think, merely to have rearranged his prejudices, so that none of them would occupy the same position in his mind that they did in his youth. . . . It would be difficult to exaggerate the extremes to which the contrast between the early and the late Wordsworth has been drawn."[22] But these charges are not supported by Burton's examination of the growth of *The Prelude,* and she notes specifically that she finds no indication of Wordsworth's having changed his mind about France; to the end, she says, he believed that the war against Napoleon was just for the same reasons that the war against revolutionary France was not.[23] And in his study of the poet's early years, George Wilbur Meyer finds many of the same ideas and overtones present in Wordsworth as early as 1793 which have been thought to characterize the works of later and apostate years.[24] Both William John Courthope and

[20] Batho, *Later Wordsworth,* pp. 117-18.

[21] Mary E. Burton, *The One Wordsworth* (Chapel Hill: University of North Carolina Press, 1942), p. 223.

[22] Ibid., pp. 52-53.

[23] Ibid., p. 67.

[24] George Wilbur Meyer, *Wordsworth's Formative Years* (Ann Arbor: University of Michigan Press, 1943), pp. 74-76. Similarly, Lindenberger, *On Wordsworth's "Prelude,"* p. 268, observes that "on close examination Wordsworth's notorious conservatism does not really look much different from his

Kenneth MacLean feel that is has not been sufficiently recognized that Wordsworth's prime political concern was always and unchangingly for individual freedom above social action.[25] Bennett Weaver sums up the feelings of those who argue against an apostasy when he says that the poet lived in trying times, and lived long; there were terror and tyranny in France and growing evil—"the rich became richer and more debased"—in England, but the poetry of Wordsworth reveals a mind always struggling and unconquerable.[26]

The foregoing summaries of the arguments attacking the charges of apostasy made against Wordsworth indicate that the *Cintra* tract, although it is an enunciation of principles central to the apostasy controversy and was written at a crucial time in the poet's life, has been largely neglected by his defenders.[27] Yet a detailed consideration of the tract is essential to a weighing of the charge of apostasy from the poet's earlier revolutionary and democratic statements. Preceding chapters of this study have offered such a consideration of *Cintra* —the circumstances and sources of information which prompted the tract, the intentions which produced it, and the principles contained in it. In particular it appears that the so-called doctrines of nationalism and leadership

---

early liberalism"—a fact, however, which Lindenberger believes the poet would have hated to admit.

[25] See Courthope, *The Liberal Movement in English Literature* (London, 1885), p. 107, and MacLean, *Agrarian Age,* p. 101.

[26] *Wordsworth: Poet of the Unconquerable Mind* (Ann Arbor: University of Michigan Press, 1965), pp. 105-9.

[27] Neglected but not totally ignored. Batho in particular acknowledges the help given her position by the commentary on the tract in Dicey's *Statesmanship of Wordsworth*—see her *Later Wordsworth,* pp. 119, 134.

157

which are sometimes supposed to mark the *Cintra* tract as a significant departure from the poet's earlier thinking are in fact in perfect harmony with previous expressions of his political and social philosophy. While not fully answering the old charge of apostasy, the understanding of the tract thus developed can at least require those who still want to make the charge to look elsewhere for the apostate's creed.

The tract, in summary, is unquestionably a strong statement of democratic faith. Wordsworth was certain that "the cause of the People ... is safe while it remains not only in the bosom but in the hands of the People" (*Cintra*, p. 155). Those who saw weakness and languishing in "the hearts of the many" were, said the poet, numerous but wholly deluded (*Cintra*, pp. 186-87). From this delusion and "imbecility" which pervaded his enemy Britain, rather than from any real power of his own, did Napoleon draw his strength; but, like all tyrants, he would yet be brought down by "his ignorance, his meanness of mind, his transports of infirm fancy, and his guilt" (*Cintra*, p. 191). For true liberty, of which the emperor's regime was a perversion, was "far mightier; and the good in human nature is stronger than the evil" (*Cintra*, p. 179).

Wordsworth's wish throughout the tract was to encourage his countrymen and their leaders to strive for higher objectives than could have entered the minds of the generals who signed the Convention of Cintra. Without minimizing military achievements, the poet set his sights on a revolutionary transformation of the peninsular nations, based on a knowledge of what truly constitutes a nation.

Regeneration and liberty were the ends he sought (*Cintra,* p. 111). "Wherever the heaving and effort of freedom was spread, purification must have followed it" (*Cintra,* pp. 115-16). He did not believe in Carlylesque heroes. Instead he believed that power corrupts, and his lament throughout the tract was that the principles and practices necessary for the revolution to which he believed that the Iberian uprisings against Napoleon should lead were held by the people but not by rulers or governments (*Cintra,* p. 126). Nevertheless, in the Peninsula, until the Convention of Cintra interfered, "the work of libera- tion was virtually accomplished," and on a more enduring basis than in the case of the French Revolution because conditions in Spain and Portugal were infinitely more favorable than they had been in France less than twenty years before (*Cintra,* p. 124; cf. pp. 176-77). At the time of the composition of the tract, just as surely as during the residence in France described in *The Prelude* (9. 123-24), Wordsworth could say:

> My heart was all
> Given to the people, and my love was theirs.[28]

The poet certainly did not expect the response to the *Cintra* tract to include charges of apostasy from his earlier principles. A month before the work was published, he wrote Francis Wrangham of his far different expecta- tions: "I am aware it will create for me a world of ene- mies, and call forth the old yell of Jacobinism."[29] In the

[28] *Prelude,* p. 321.

[29] *Letters: Middle Years,* 1:290. As shown in the preceding chapter, this ex- pectation was at least partly justified by the response to the tract of those who

tract itself he had stressed the continuity of his principles. He put himself among those—"an immense majority
of the people of Great Britian"—who had "most
eagerly opposed the war" against revolutionary France
in 1793 but who, in their continuing hostility to tyranny
and lawless ambition, had later been obliged to recognize
Napoleonic France as their enemy (*Cintra*, p. 8). Of
these people, himself included, he wrote: "Their conduct
was herein consistent: they proved that they kept their
eyes steadily fixed upon principles" (*Cintra*, p. 8).
The same sorrowful recognition that adherence to principles required a change from opposing the war to
enthusiastically endorsing it appears in *The Prelude*
(11. 206 - 17):

> But now, become oppressors in their turn,
> Frenchmen had changed a war of self - defence
> For one of conquest, losing sight of all
> Which they had struggled for: now mounted up,
> Openly in the eye of earth and heaven,
> The scale of liberty. I read her doom,
> With anger vexed, with disappointment sore,
> But not dismayed, nor taking to the shame
> Of a false prophet. While resentment rose
> Striving to hide, what nought could heal, the wounds
> Of mortified presumption, I adhered
> More firmly to old tenets.[30]

---

disliked it (or its author). The "old yell" was to be raised, paradoxically, in
the poet's defense by W. H. White, *Examination of the Charge of Apostasy,*
p. 19, who declares that Wordsworth showed himself still a Jacobin at heart
not only in the tract but in the addresses to the freeholders of Westmoreland
in 1818.
[30] *Prelude,* p. 413. This is the reading of the 1850 *Prelude,* but the earliest
Prelude, composed several years before *Cintra,* says substantially the same

Most especially in the conquest of Switzerland did Napoleon earn the beginnings of Wordsworth's hatred. It was the freedom of that land which the poet had hailed as early as 1791 and 1792 in "Descriptive Sketches."[31] In his sonnet "Thought of a Briton on the Subjugation of Switzerland," he expressed the hope that his country could learn from the sad experience with invading tyranny of the still greatly admired Swiss:

> Two voices are there; one is of the sea,
> One of the mountains; each a mighty Voice:
> In both from age to age thou didst rejoice,
> They were thy chosen music, Liberty!
> There came a Tyrant, and with holy glee
> Thou fought'st against him; but hast vainly striven:
> Thou from thy Alpine holds at length art driven,
> Where not a torrent murmurs heard by thee.
> Of one deep bliss thine ear hath been bereft:
> Then cleave, O cleave to that which still is left;
> For, high-souled Maid, what sorrow would it be
> That Mountain floods should thunder as before,
> And Ocean bellow from his rocky shore,
> And neither awful Voice be heard by thee![32]

The same feeling, linked with a regretful recognition that the poet could not adhere to the same policy he had favored before the French invasion of Switzerland and still maintain his principles, is expressed almost at the be-

---

thing—cf. p. 412.
[31] *Poetical Works,* 1:74.
[32] Ibid., 3:115.

ginning of the tract (*Cintra,* p. 8). Wordsworth's change
of attitude toward France did not constitute apostasy. It
was the French who apostatized.[33] The successive dis-
appointments from the Reign of Terror to the Convention
of Cintra only made the poet adhere "more firmly to old
tenets."[34]

He did change his mind about Sir Arthur Wellesley, but
in circumstances similar, though in a reverse direction,
to his changing opinion of France. To Coleridge in May,
1809, at the time of the publication of the tract, the poet
wrote of his dread of the common disposition to forgive
and relent in cases of public offense like Wellesley's in
Portugal. He feared that with Wellesley back in the Peninsula, one victory "would blot out all remembrance of
his former transactions," and the public would be deluded
into thinking there was a change in the general's moral
spirit.[35] The later successes of Wellesley, by then duke
of Wellington, seem, however, to have been accompanied,
at least in Wordsworth's mind, by a genuine moral regeneration. The poet did not forget the Convention of Cintra,
but he came to admire the general. To Henry Reed, his
American editor, who urged the poet to reprint the *Cintra* tract, Wordsworth wrote of these mixed feelings in
1840:

[33] The English Whigs must be included as apostates in the same sense for
failing to oppose France when France opposed liberty. See Dicey, *Statesmanship of Wordsworth,* p. 107.
[34] *Prelude* (bk. 11, line 217), p. 413. His early letter in defense of the French
Revolution to the bishop of Llandaff also seems to have been associated
strongly in Wordsworth's mind with the tract in defense of the Iberian rebellions at the time of the composition of the latter—see *Letters: Middle Years,*
1:296.
[35] *Letters: Middle Years,* 1:306.

I am much pleased by what you say . . . upon the
tract of the Convention of Cintra, & I think myself
with some interest upon its being reprinted hereafter,
along with my other writings. But the respect, which
in common with all the rest of the rational part of
the world, I bear for the Duke of Wellington, will
prevent my reprinting the pamphlet during his life-
time. It has not been in my power to read the Volumes
of his Despatches which I hear so highly spoken of,
but I am convinced that nothing they contain could
alter my opinion of the injurious tendency of that, or
any other Convention, conducted upon such Principles. [36]

Wordsworth himself believed that in all his works he
was always firm and consistent in his principles. And he
was sensitive to what he considered to be unjust charges
of apostasy. To James Losh, whom he called a "candid
and enlightened Friend," the poet wrote in 1821 in answer
to a question regarding "a supposed change in my Political opinions":

I should think that I had lived to little purpose if
my notions on the subject of Government had undergone no modification—my youth must, in that case,
have been without enthusiasm, and my manhood en-
dued with small capability of profiting by reflexion.
If I were addressing those who have dealt so liberally
with the words Renegado Apostate, etc., I should

[36] *Wordsworth and Reed: The Poet's Correspondence with His American
Editor, 1836-1850,* ed. Leslie Nathan Broughton (Ithaca: Cornell University
Press, 1933), p. 36.

retort the charge upon them, and say, *you* have
been deluded by *Places* and *Persons,* while I have
stuck to *Principles—I* abandoned France, and her
Rulers, when *they* abandoned the struggle for Liberty, gave themselves up to Tyranny, and endeavoured
to enslave the world. I disapproved of the war against
France at its commencement, thinking ... that it
might have been avoided—but after Buonaparte had
violated the Independence of Switzerland, my heart
turned against him, and against the Nation that could
submit to be the Instrument of such an outrage. Here
it was that I parted, in feeling, from the Whigs, and
to a certain degree united with their Adversaries,
who were free from the delusion (such I must ever
regard it) of Mr Fox and his Party, that a safe and
honourable Peace was practicable with the French
nation.... Therefore, to aim at the overthrow of
that inordinate Ambition by War, I sided with the
Ministry, not from general approbation of their Conduct, but as men who thought right on this essential
point. How deeply this question interested me will
be plain to any one who will take the trouble of reading my political Sonnets, and the Tract occasioned
by the "Convention of Cintra," in which are sufficient
evidences of my dissatisfaction with the mode of
conducting the war, and a prophetic display of the
course which it would take if carried on upon the
principles of justice, and with due respect for the
feelings of the oppressed nations.[37]

[37] *Letters: Later Years,* 1:56-57.

Wordsworth in later years never changed his mind about either the Convention of Cintra or the principles he had expressed in the *Cintra* tract. For its author neither the tract nor any of his later works represented a departure from his early position among "that odious class of men called democrats" in which he had vowed to continue forever.[38] The political principles of the *Cintra* tract, often reiterated by Wordsworth in later years, are also consistent, as he intended them to be, with his earlier expressions of views on political and social philosophy. "A dirge devoutly breathed o'er sorrows past,"[39] the *Cintra* tract, by no means the creed of an apostate, is a great monument to the continuity of Wordsworth's principles.

[38] *Early Letters,* pp. 115-16.
[39] *Poetical Works,* 3:129.

Selected Bibliography

＜＿＿＿＞

WRITINGS OF WORDSWORTH

The Early Letters of William and Dorothy Wordsworth (1785-1805). Edited by Ernest de Selincourt. London: Oxford University Press, 1935.

The Letters of William and Dorothy Wordsworth: The Middle Years. Edited by Ernest de Selincourt. 2 vols. Oxford: Oxford University Press, 1937.

The Letters of William and Dorothy Wordsworth: The Later Years. Edited by Ernest de Selincourt. 3 vols. Oxford: Oxford University Press, 1939.

Memoirs of William Wordsworth. Edited by Christopher Wordsworth. 2 vols. Boston, 1851.

The Poetical Works of William Wordsworth. Edited by Ernest de Selincourt and Helen Darbishire. 2d ed. rev. 5 vols. Oxford: Oxford University Press, 1952-59.

Political Tracts of Wordsworth, Coleridge and Shelley. Edited by R. J. White. Cambridge: Cambridge University Press, 1953.

The Prelude, or Growth of a Poet's Mind. Edited by Ernest de Selincourt. 2d ed. revised by Helen Darbishire. Oxford: Oxford University Press, 1959.

The Prose Works of William Wordsworth. Edited by Alexander B. Grosart. 3 vols. London: E. Moxon, Son, and Co., 1876.

Prose Works of William Wordsworth. Edited by William Knight. 2 vols. London, 1896.

Wordsworth and Reed: The Poet's Correspondence with His American Editor, 1836-1850. Edited by Leslie Nathan Broughton. Ithaca: Cornell University Press, 1933.

Wordsworth's Tract on the Convention of Cintra, with Two Letters of Wordsworth Written in the Year 1811. Edited by A. V. Dicey. London: Oxford University Press, 1915.

WRITINGS OF WORDSWORTH'S CONTEMPORARIES

Coleridge, Samuel Taylor. *Collected Letters of Samuel Taylor Coleridge*. Edited by Earl Leslie Griggs. 4 vols. Oxford: Oxford University Press, 1956-59.

Coleridge, Sara. *Memoir and Letters of Sara Coleridge*. Edited by Edith Coleridge. New York, 1874.

Hazlitt, William. *The Life of Napoleon Buonaparte*. 4 vols. London, 1852.

Hunt, Leigh. *Leigh Hunt's Political and Occasional Essays*. Edited by Lawrence Huston Houtchens and Carolyn Washburn Houtchens. New York: Columbia University Press, 1962.

Lamb, Charles, and Lamb, Mary. *The Works of Charles and Mary Lamb*. Edited by E. V. Lucas. 7 vols. New York: G. P. Putnam's Sons, 1905.

Lockhart, John Gibson. *Memoirs of the Life of Sir Walter Scott.* 5 vols. Boston: Macmillan Co., 1902.

Moore, James. *A Narrative of the Campaign of the British Army in Spain.* London, 1809.

Napier, W. F. P. *History of the War in the Peninsula and in the South of France.* 5 vols. New York: Franklin Hudson Publishers, 1856.

Robinson, Henry Crabb. *Blake, Coleridge, Wordsworth, Lamb, Etc., Being Selections from the Remains of Henry Crabb Robinson.* Edited by Edith J. Morley. New York: Longmans Green & Co., 1922.

———. *The Correspondence of Henry Crabb Robinson with the Wordsworth Circle.* Edited by Edith J. Morley. 2 vols. Oxford: Oxford University Press, 1927.

———. *Henry Crabb Robinson on Books and Their Writers.* Edited by Edith J. Morley. 3 vols. London: J. M. Dent & Sons, 1938.

Scott, Sir Walter. *The Life of Napoleon Buonaparte, Emperor of the French.* 2 vols. Philadelphia, 1854.

Southey, Robert. *History of the Peninsular War.* 2 vols. London, n.d.

———. *The Life and Correspondence of Robert Southey.* Edited by Charles Cuthbert Southey. 4 vols. London, 1850.

———. *New Letters of Robert Southey.* Edited by Kenneth Curry. 2 vols. New York: Columbia University Press, 1965.

———. *Selections from the Letters of Robert Southey.* Edited by John Wood Warter. 4 vols. London, 1856.

PERIODICALS

Courier (London), September 1808-January 1809.

Edinburgh Annual Register, 1808.

Edinburgh Review, July 1809-January 1810.

Gaceta de Madrid, September 1808.

Observer (London), September 1808.

"Relation des événemens d'Espagne," *Gazette nationale et Moniteur* (Paris), 5 September 1808, pp. 979-83.

Times (London), July 1808-November 1808.

HISTORICAL AND CRITICAL STUDIES

Batho, Edith C. *The Later Wordsworth.* Cambridge: Cambridge University Press, 1933.

Beatty, Arthur. *William Wordsworth: His Doctrine and Art in Their Historical Relations.* Madison: University of Wisconsin Press, 1962.

Bernbaum, Ernest. *Guide through the Romantic Movement.* New York: Ronald Press Co., 1949.

Brandes, George. *Main Currents in Nineteenth Century Literature.* 5 vols. New York: Boni & Liveright, 1905.

Brinton, Crane. *Political Ideas of the English Romanticists.* London: Oxford University Press, 1926.

Burton, Mary E. *The One Wordsworth.* Chapel Hill: University of North Carolina Press, 1942.

Carnall, Geoffrey. *Robert Southey and His Age: The Development of a Conservative Mind.* Oxford: Oxford University Press, 1960.

Chew, Samuel C. *The Nineteenth Century and After.* Vol. 4 of *A Literary History of England,* edited by Albert C. Baugh. New York: Appleton-Century-Crofts, 1948.

Churchill, Winston S. *A History of the English-Speaking Peoples: The Age of Revolution.* London: Cassell and Co., 1957.

Cobban, Alfred. *Edmund Burke and the Revolt against the Eighteenth Century.* 2d ed. London: George Allen & Unwin, 1960.

Courthope, William John. *The Liberal Movement in English Literature.* London, 1885.

Dicey, A. V. *The Statesmanship of Wordsworth.* Oxford: Oxford University Press, 1917.

Elwin, Malcolm. *The First Romantics.* New York: Longmans, Green & Co., 1948.

Fink, Z. S. "Wordsworth and the English Republican Tradition." *Journal of English and Germanic Philology* 47 (1948): 107-26.

Graham, Walter. "The Politics of the Greater Romantic Poets." *PMLA* 36 (1921): 60-78.

Grierson, Herbert J. C. *Milton and Wordsworth.* New York: Macmillan Co., 1937.

Hamilton, Carson C. *Wordsworth's Decline in Poetic Power: Prophet into High Priest.* New York: Exposition Press, 1963.

Harper, George McLean. *William Wordsworth: His Life, Works, and Influence.* 2 vols. New York: Charles Scribner's Sons, 1923.

Havens, Raymond D. "A Project of Wordsworth's." *Review of English Studies* 5 (1929): 320-22.

Hawkes, C. P. "The Spanish Adventure of Walter Savage

Landor." *Cornhill Magazine*, n.s. 74 (1933): 551-64.

Herford, C. H. *Wordsworth*. London: George Routledge & Sons, 1930.

Hildebrandt, Josephine Elizabeth. "Wordsworth's Prose." Master's thesis, Tulane University, 1928.

Jordan, John E. *De Quincey to Wordsworth: A Biography of a Relationship*. Berkeley and Los Angeles: University of California Press, 1962.

Knight, William. *The Life of William Wordsworth*. 3 vols. Edinburgh, 1889.

Legouis, Emile. *The Early Life of William Wordsworth*. Translated by J. W. Matthews. New York: E. P. Dutton & Co., 1918.

Lehman, B. H. *Carlyle's Theory of the Hero: Its Sources, Development, History, and Influence on Carlyle's Work*. Durham: Duke University Press, 1928.

———. "The Doctrine of Leadership in the Greater Romantic Poets." *PMLA* 37 (1922): 639-61.

Lindenberger, Herbert. *On Wordsworth's "Prelude."* Princeton: Princeton University Press, 1963.

Logan, James Venable. *Wordsworthian Criticism: A Guide and Bibliography*. Columbus: Ohio State University Press, 1947.

MacLean, Kenneth. *Agrarian Age: A Background for Wordsworth*. New Haven: Yale University Press, 1950.

Madariaga, Salvador de. *Shelley and Calderon and Other Essays on English and Spanish Poetry*. London: Constable & Co., 1920.

Maxwell, W. H. *The Victories of Wellington and the British Armies*. London, 1891.

Mendez Bejarano, Mario. *Historia de los afrancesados.*

Madrid: Impresa de Felipe Peña Cruz, 1912.

Meyer, George Wilbur. *Wordsworth's Formative Years.* Ann Arbor: University of Michigan Press, 1943.

Moorman, Mary. *William Wordsworth, a Biography: The Later Years, 1803-1850.* Oxford: Oxford University Press, 1965.

Pinheiro Chagas, Manuel. *Historia de Portugal.* 14 vols. Lisbon: Empreza da Historia de Portugal, 1899-1909.

Queipo de Llano, José María. *Historia del levantamiento, guerra y revolución de España.* Madrid: Editorial Hernando, 1926.

Raleigh, Walter. *Wordsworth.* London: E. Arnold, 1903.

Rannie, David Watson. *Wordsworth and His Circle.* New York: G. P. Putnam's Sons, 1907.

Read, Herbert. *Wordsworth.* New York: Peter Smith, 1931.

Renwick, W. L. *English Literature, 1789-1815.* Oxford History of English Literature, edited by F. P. Wilson and Bonamy Dobrée, vol. 9. Oxford: Oxford University Press, 1963.

Rose, J. Holland. *Nationality in Modern History.* New York: Macmillan Co., 1916.

San Juan, Ernest, Jr. "Wordsworth and Political Commitment." *Dalhousie Review* 45 (1965): 299-306.

Shand, Alexander Innes. *The War in the Peninsula, 1808-1814.* New York, 1898.

Smith, Elsie. *An Estimate of William Wordsworth by His Contemporaries, 1793-1822.* Oxford: Basil Blackwell & Mott, 1932.

Smith, James Cruickshanks. *A Study of Wordsworth.* 2d ed. rev. Edinburgh: Oliver & Boyd, 1946.

Sperry, Willard L. *Wordsworth's Anti-Climax.* Cambridge: Harvard University Press, 1935.

Strout, A. L. "Wordsworth's Dessication." *Modern Language Review* 35 (1940): 162-72.

Todd, Francis Murray. *Politics and the Poet: A Study of Wordsworth.* London: Methuen & Co., 1957.

Ward, A. W., and Gooch, G. P., eds. *The Cambridge History of British Foreign Policy.* 3 vols. New York: Macmillan Co., 1922-23.

Weaver, Bennett. *Wordsworth: Poet of the Unconquerable Mind.* Ann Arbor: University of Michigan Press, 1965.

Wells, John Edwin. "De Quincey's Punctuation of Wordsworth's *Cintra.*" *Times Literary Supplement,* 3 November 1932, p. 815.

———. "Printer's Bills for Coleridge's *Friend* and Wordsworth's *Cintra.*" *Studies in Philology* 36 (1939): 521-23.

———. "The Story of Wordsworth's *Cintra.*" *Studies in Philology* 18 (1921): 15-76.

White, W. Hale. *An Examination of the Charge of Apostasy against Wordsworth.* London, 1898.

Woodring, Carl R. "On Liberty in the Poetry of Wordsworth." *PMLA* 70 (1955): 1033-48.

Worthington, Jane. *Wordsworth's Reading of Roman Prose.* New Haven: Yale University Press, 1946.

Wylie, Laura Johnson. "The Social Philosophy of Wordsworth." *Social Studies in English Literature,* pp. 117-65. Boston: Houghton Mifflin Co., 1916.

Index

Allen Bank, 5, 36, 46, 51

American Revolution, 91

Andalusia, 79

Andrade, Bernardine Freire de, 26

Archimedes, 126 n

Asturias, 80

Austria, 98

Bailén, battle of, 13, 14, 15, 70, 80

Batho, Edith, 155-56, 157 n

Baylen. See Bailén

Beaumont, Lady Margaret, 143

Beaupuy, Michel, 62 n

Bedford, Grosvenor, 31

Biscay, 126

Bonaparte, Joseph, 14, 27, 144

Bonaparte, Napoleon, 95 and n, 97, 103, 105, 108, 144, 152; as ruling power in Spain and Portugal, 3, 4, 8, 12, 13, 19, 76-78; strengths and weaknesses as leader, 82, 98, 114, 127-30, 132-33, 158; Wordsworth's opinion of, 6-7, 87, 94, 145

Burke, Edmund, 62 n, 137, 138, 139; *Reflections on the Revolution in France,* 145

Burrard, Harry, 17, 23, 26, 28, 34-35, 37, 60

Burton, Mary E., 156

Byron, Lord, *Childe Harold's Pilgrimage,* 22 n

Calvert (Southey's friend), 41

Canning, George, 4, 12, 143

Carlyle, Thomas, 111-12, 115, 116, 117, 120, 122, 159

Carnall, Geoffrey, 59

Carthage, 105, 126

Castaños, Francisco Javier, 13

Castlereagh, Robert, and Tory ministry: and court of inquiry, 74-75, 122 (*see also* court of inquiry, following Convention of Cintra); intervention in Peninsula, 4, 32, 57, 145, 164; involvement in Convention of Cintra, 21, 44-45, 88-89, 92-93, 121-22

Charles IV of Spain, 3

Chew, Samuel, 111, 113, 114, 154

Childe Harold's Pilgrimage (Byron), 22 n

Churchill, Winston, 13, 81

Cicero, 62 n

Cid, The, 126

Cintra, 21, 22. *See also* Convention of Cintra

Clarke, Mary Ann, 141

Clarkson, Catherine, 45, 46, 50, 135-36, 136 n

Cobban, Alfred, 153-54

Coleridge, Derwent, 47

Coleridge, Hartley, 47

Coleridge, Henry Nelson, 49 n

Coleridge, Samuel Taylor, 37, 46, 48, 145, 162; *The Friend,* 37; involvement in composition of *Cintra* tract, 10 n, 44, 48-49, 49 n, 62 n; opinion of *Cintra* tract, 55-56, 94, 135, 139-40 and n; reaction to Convention of Cintra, 11, 36, 42, 43

Coleridge, Sara (daughter of Samuel), 36

Coleridge, Sara (wife of Samuel), 46

Convention of Cintra: as example of violated principles, 29, 60-84, 91, 130, 131, 132; reaction of public to, 26-29, 32-36, 39, 44-45, 48-49, 54, 92-94, 141; reaction of Wordsworth circle to, 35-44; signed, 21; terms of, 22-25, 122, 123

Convention of Cintra (Wordsworth); as statement of principles, not historical record, 59-84, 159-60, 164-65; called apostate, 154-58; composition of, 7, 12, 32, 43-58, 63; contemporary opinions of, 94, 135-44; doctrine of leadership in, 64, 111-32, 159;

doctrine of National Happiness in, 64, 85-110, 146, 158-59; *nation* defined in, 88-94; publication of, 11, 37-38, 47-58; results of, 144-49

Corbett, P. S., 28

Coruña, battle of, 35, 122

Cotton, Charles, 15, 66

Courier (London), 11, 15, 16, 17, 18, 21-26, 39, 63-64; *Cintra* published in, 48-50, 136

Courthope, William John, 156-57

court of inquiry, following Convention of Cintra, 28, 33n, 34, 39, 40, 41, 44, 63, 72-75, 122-23, 130

Crabbe, George, 37

Cromwell, Oliver, 39

Crosthwaite, 42

Dalrymple, Hew, 23, 26, 28, 35, 37, 40, 60

De Quincey, Thomas, 10n, 18n, 36, 46, 50-58, 63, 76, 135, 140, 142

de Selincourt, Ernest, 8

Dicey, A. V., 59, 68, 81, 86-87, 94-95n, 106n, 145, 157n

Doblado Bookstore (Madrid), 144

Dreadnought, H.M.S., 39n

Dupont, Pierre, 13, 14, 70

Dyce, Alexander, 49n

Edinburgh Review, 12, 25, 35

Elvas, 34

Elwin, Malcolm, 151-52

Embassy of Portugal in London, 141-42 and n

Embassy of Spain in London, 141-43 and n

Empedocles, 126n

Examiner (Leigh Hunt), 12, 26, 114

Fenwick, Isabella, 5, 9

Ferdinand VII of Spain, 3, 37

Ferrol, El, 122

Feu, Magalhães, 142n

Flower, Benjamin, 57

French Revolution, 3, 4, 5, 6, 17, 35, 57, 91, 120-21, 159

Friend, The (Coleridge), 37

Gaceta (Madrid), 27

Galluzo, General, 34

Garibaldi, Giuseppe, 87

Gazette nationale et Moniteur (Paris), 17, 18n

generals, British, at Convention of Cintra. *See* Burrard, Harry; Dalrymple, Hew; Wellesley, Arthur

George III of England, 4, 12, 15, 16, 39, 42, 45

Germany, unification of, 107, 107-108n, 109

Gifford, William, 34

Graham, Walter, 154

Grasmere, 5, 37, 51, 54, 63

Hamilton, Carson C., 153

Harrington, James, 62n

Havens, Raymond D., 28

Hazlitt, William, 28, 35n

Herford, C. H., 152n

History of Portugal (Southey), 42

History of the Peninsular War (Southey), 82-84, 132-33

Hofer, Andrew, 115

Hope, John, 34

Hunt, Leigh, 115, *Examiner,* 12, 26, 114

Hutchinson, Sara, 46, 57-58

Iberian Peninsula. *See under* names of cities and provinces of Spain and Portugal

Inquisition, 3, 37

International Brigades (in Spanish Civil War), 31-32

Italy, unification of, 107, 107-108n, 109

Jacobinism, 159, 160n

John VI, Prince Regent of Portugal, 3, 15, 16, 18, 19, 20

Jordan, John E., 54

Junot, Andoche, 15, 16, 18, 19, 20, 22, 24n, 27, 40, 60, 70

Keswick, 6

Lamb, Charles, 137 and n

Landor, Walter Savage, 32, 38, 43

leadership, doctrine of. *See Convention of Cintra,* doctrine of leadership in

Lehman, B. H., 111-13, 114, 116, 154

Leon, 126

Life of Napoleon Buonaparte (Scott), 33-34

Lindenberger, Herbert, 140, 157-58n

Lisbon, 14, 15, 16, 20, 21, 24, 27, 68

Livy, 62n

London Observer, 25, 26

London Review, 139

Lonsdale, William, Earl of, 42

Losh, James, 163

Louis XVIII of France, 24n

Mac Lean, Kenneth, 146, 157

Madariaga, Salvador de, 143n

Madrid, 14, 27, 122

Madrid Junta, 3, 27

Marathon, battle of, 62

Mathews, William, 7, 151

Mazzini, Giuseppe, 86, 87

Méndez Bejarano, Mario, 144

Meyer, George Wilbur, 156

Milton, John, 62n, 94, 111, 125, 137n, 140

Ministry of Foreign Affairs (Madrid), 143n

Moore, John, 35, 54, 114, 115, 122, 124

Moorman, Mary, 5, 137n, 147

Morning Post (London), 6, 9

Napier, W. F. P., 27, 59, 68, 102n

Napoleon. *See* Bonaparte, Napoleon

National Happiness, doctrine of. *See Convention of Cintra,* doctrine of National Happiness in

nationalism. *See Convention of Cintra,* doctrine of National Happiness in

Obidos, 15

Oporto, Bishop of, 27

Oviedo, 101

Palafox, José de, 126n, 126-27

Pasley, Charles William, 95, 99, 103, 105, 107, 108, 109

Pelayo, 126

Plutarch, 62n

Poole, Thomas, 51

Prince Regent of Portugal. *See* John VI, Prince Regent of Portugal

protest meetings: in City of London, 39, 41, 44, 71, 75; in Lake Counties, 40-44

Prussia, 98

Pyrenees, 76

Quarterly Review, 34

Quayle, Thomas, 138

Queipo de Llana, José María, 4n

Raise-gap, 5, 8

Raleigh, Walter, 155

Read, Herbert, 87, 154

Reed, Henry, 162-63

Reflections on the Revolution in France (Burke), 145

Robinson, Anthony, 137 and n

Robinson, Henry Crabb, 12, 83, 136, 137, 138-39 and n, 152

Robinson, Thomas, 136

Rogers, Samuel, 37

Rome, 105, 126

Rousseau, Jean-Jacques, 62n

Russia, 109

Rydal Mount, 156

Saint Jerome Bible, 24n

Salamanca, 80

San Juan, Ernest, Jr., 153

Saragossa, 80, 126 and n

Scipio, 105

Scott, Sir Walter, 31, 34, 39, 114, 115, 136, 140, 145; *Life of Napoleon Buonaparte,* 33-34

Senhouse, Humphrey, 40

Seville, 13, 79, 144

Shand, Alexander Innes, 28

Sharpe, Richard, 36

Sheridan, Richard Brinsley, 4, 12

Smith, Elsie, 138-39n

Smith, J. C., 87-88

Smith, Thomas W., 10n

Southey, Robert, 10n, 32, 33n, 58, 98, 136, 140n; *History of Portugal,* 42; *History of the Peninsular War,* 82-84, 132-33; reaction to Convention of Cintra, 31, 36, 38, 40-44

Southey, Tom, 39n, 42, 43, 63n

Spedding (Southey's friend), 40-41

Sperry, Willard L., 154-55

Stuart, Daniel, 11, 48, 49, 52, 53, 55-58, 61, 135

Switzerland, French invasion of, 161, 164

Sydney, Algernon, 62n

Tell, William, 115

Theocritus, 126n

Thermopylae, battle of, 62

Tilli, General, 13

Times (London), 12, 13, 14, 16, 17, 21-28, 39, 70

Timoleon, 126n

Toda, Eduardo, 142-43n

Todd, F. M., 152

Tories. *See* Castlereagh, Robert, and Tory ministry

Valencia, 80
Vallon, Annette, 154
Vimeiro, battle of, 16, 49, 68, 114
Vizcaya. *See* Biscay

Watson, Bishop of Llandaff, 57. *See also* Wordsworth, William "Apology for the French Revolution, 1793" (letter to Bishop Watson of Llandaff)
Weaver, Bennett, 157
Wellesley, Arthur, 37, 114; commander in Spain and Portugal, 5, 14, 15-17, 18, 20, 35, 57; negotiator of Convention of Cintra, 23, 24, 25-28, 64-66, 68, 146; Wordsworth's opinions of, 59-60, 124-25, 132-33, 162-63
Wellington, Duke of. *See* Wellesley, Arthur
Wells, John Edwin, 48, 53, 56
Whigs, 12, 17, 35 and n, 162n, 164
White, R. J., 140n

White, William Hale, 155, 160n
Wilson, John, 145
World War I, 86-87, 95n
Wordsworth, Christopher, 147
Wordsworth, Dorothy, 45, 46, 47, 53, 135, 143, 152
Wordsworth, Mary Hutchinson, 46, 47, 53-55
Wordsworth, William: "Apology for the French Revolution, 1793" (letter to Bishop Watson of Llandaff), 57, 85, 112-14, 116, 155, 162n; "Calais, August, 1802," 6; *Cintra* tract *(see Convention of Cintra);* "Composed at the Same Time and on the Same Occasion" ("I dropped my pen; and listened to the Wind"), 147, 148-49, 165; "Composed While the Author Was Engaged in Writing a Tract Occasioned by the Convention of Cintra" ("Not mid the World's vain objects that enslave"), 147-48; *Concerning the Relations of Great Britain, Spain, and Portugal . . . (see*

Convention of Cintra); "Descriptive Sketches," 161; "1811" ("The power of Armies is a visable thing"), 89-90; "1810" ("Ah! where is Palafox?"), 127; "1810" ("O'erweening Statesmen have full long relied"), 80-81; *The Excursion,* 99-100, 153; "Great men have been among us" (sonnet), 125; "Hofer," 115; "Indignation of a High-Minded Spaniard," 32, 76-77; "London, 1802" ("Milton! thou shouldst be living at this hour"), 125; "Michael," 79; "Pelayo," 7-8; "Poems Dedicated to National Independence and Liberty," 32; *The Prelude,* 115, 125-26, 151, 156, 159, 160; "Resolution and Independence," 79; "Spanish Guerillas," 32; "Thought of a Briton on the Subjugation of Switzerland," 6, 161; "When I Have Borne in Memory," 9; "Written in London, September, 1802" ("Oh Friend! I know not which way I must look"), 5, 9

Worthington, Jane, 99

Wrangham, Francis, 37, 45, 47, 137n, 141, 159

York, Duke of, 141, 146-47

Zaragoza. *See* Saragossa